Praise for *Women of True Grit*

"From board rooms to sports fields, from sex therapists to the army, education
to banking, Tina Savas and Edie Hand honor brilliant achieving "Second Wave"
feminists in their inspiring book. Some of their heroes were political activists who
forged the way for all women to achieve. Others, professionals whose success was
accomplished because of the work of the activists (as well as to their own smarts,
drive and determination), advanced the possibilities for all women. They are
products of a great generation of American women who continued the fight for
complete equality and opportunity for all women."

—Jacqui Ceballos
Founder/President Veteran Feminists of America

"I want to thank Edie and Tina for highlighting the great contributions of these
women to our nation and culture. Through these examples in their book—we see
from a unique perspective the qualities of strength, determination, and yet grace,
which have marked the success of these great Americans. I believe everyone, no
doubt, will enjoy reading about the figures that they have included who have such
a myriad of qualities and experiences."

—U.S. Congressman Robert B. Aderholt
Alabama's Fourth Congressional District

"Perseverance: No matter how tough the job, you don't give up.
True Grit is perseverance."

—Wilma L. Vaught
Brigadier General USAF Retired,
President of Women's Memorial Foundation, Washington D.C.

For Becky Joi

WOMEN
OF TRUE GRIT

Intimate. Informative. Inspirational.

Thank you for all you do for women everywhere. Enjoy!

40 phenomenal women share real life stories
with secrets to success for all generations.

EDIE HAND & TINA SAVAS

*Tina Savas*

**Canterbury House Publishing**

Vilas, North Carolina

Canterbury House Publishing, Ltd.
in partnership with Edie Hand and Tina Savas
www.ediehand.com   www.womenoftruegrit.com
www.canterburyhousepublishing.com

For information about permission to reproduce
selections from this book, write to:
Permissions
Attention: Edie Hand/Tina Savas
800 Highway 78 E PMB 403
Jasper, AL 35501-3936
or
Canterbury House Publishing, Ltd.
225 Ira Harmon Rd.
Vilas, NC 28692-9369

Book design by Aaron Burleson, Spokesmedia
Photography by Chris Savas | www.chrissavas.com

Library of Congress Cataloging-in-Publication Data

Hand, Edie, 1951-
Women of true grit / by Edie Hand and Tina Savas.
    p. cm.
ISBN 978-0-9825396-0-6
1. Women--Biography. 2. Success--Case studies. 3. Self-realization in
women--Case studies. 4. Women in the professions--Biography. 5.
Businesswomen--Biography. 6. Women entertainers--Biography. I. Savas,
Tina. II. Title.

HQ1123.H36 2010
305.43092'2--dc22
[B]

2009053493

Second Printing May 2010

*Author's Note: Sources for some quotes were taken from the Internet.
These are public domain quotes.*

Dedication

"Lucille (Ariniello) Luongo was a mentor and friend to me. She shared the vision of this book and touched my heart with a forever spirit with her acts of kindness toward others. Lucille was born May 29, 1948, and lost her battle with lung cancer on January 11th, 2006. She was a woman of many accomplishments. She was True Grit."

—Edie Hand Aldridge

"For my mother, Kitty Zaden Verciglio—the strongest, most solid woman I have ever known. She was always there for me, sharing my strengths and weaknesses, and then, showing me how to use them to achieve anything of worth. Her faith in me was endless and I only wish she had lived to read this book. She was my Number One."

—Tina Verciglio Savas

We also wish to dedicate this book to all mothers who have had the ***True Grit*** to raise young women who dared to blaze a path to inspire and encourage us to follow our dreams of unimaginable heights.

—Edie & Tina

Acknowledgment

This book began as two separate books but a common goal to share voices of women of great worth. As co-authors, we would like to thank *each other* for having the foresight and ability to work together to create *Women of True Grit*.

Special thanks to the following for helping make this book a reality Wendy Dingwall of *Canterbury House Publishing*, who believed in our mission; Bob Layne of The Visibility Company, who was such a force in the creativity of *Women of True Grit* from the concept; Harvey Klinger, thank you for being such a support as a literary agent; Sandra Horton, our tireless editor extraordinaire; Chris Savas of *Photography by Chris Savas* for our wonderful book jacket photo; Dr. David Basilico for his invaluable advice; Lynn Cushing, who was there every step of the way; Kristi Poss for her extraordinary typing skills; and Elena Difiore & Barbara Dury, the dream team for research of such women of worth. So many special women made contributions to our book like Prill Boyle, Gail Small, Judith Murray, Judy Nelon, Edna Lopez, and Galina J. Fouks-Abele to name a few. Many thanks go to the American City Business Journal publishers and Chambers of Commerce throughout the country, as well as SCORE (Service Corps of Retired Executives) and Women Business Center directors. Thank you to all those other friends and supporters who stood by us and offered help along the way....you know who you are!

We would like to express our heartfelt thanks to Barbara Mandrell for her insightful *Foreword*.

Our sincerest appreciation extends to Dr. Maya Angelou for supporting our book and lending her perfect poem, *Phenomenal Woman*, for these women of true grit.

And last but never least, we want to extend a very special thank you to our families...to our husbands Mark Aldridge and Paul Savas, and our sons Linc Hand and Alex Savas. Without your love and constant presence, our dream would never have materialized into this book.

With warmest regards,
Edie & Tina

Foreword

Imagine that you are among the women who have achieved success in your particular field of expertise. Where would you be now if it weren't for the women who came before you?

Many of the women in this book recorded firsts in their respective fields and are still with us today, able and willing to share their stories with Edie Hand and Tina Savas. Their hope is that you will come away with knowledge that can be used and passed on.

This is what matters most to these women.

Their experiences go beyond these pages. You may have found yourselves in at least a couple of the situations you will read about in this book. We finally get to hear what it was *really* like to blaze a trail or break a glass ceiling. Though some of the experiences are hard to believe, they are all real.

These women pioneers...*who are still pioneering*...carry the torch that past generations of women worked so hard to light. They open their hearts in these pages. In unison, they believe women will advance more quickly if they truly understand their past. History or *herstory*, it must be told...deep words of history to lend an understanding of the meaning of *True Grit* and what it took for these women to become the best of the best. These women lived it, persevered and are still succeeding despite all odds against them.

It is important not to forget.

These secrets of success provide insight for both women and men. My hope is that you will appreciate the vulnerability of these women and see it as their strength. These stories will inspire the drive and inner courage needed to believe in oneself.

Even though many of these women are retired, they still feel deeply connected to women's struggles and challenges today. They make a difference in all walks of life. Some are involved in politics, some are entertainers or entrepreneurs, and others are involved in non-profit work, forming their own foundations. Whatever the case, they will always work to advance the status of women in the world. And they will always be an inspiration to us all.

You will love these women of TRUE GRIT and be thankful for their great worth!

—Barbara Mandrell
Recording Artist, Actress and Author of
*New York Times **Best Seller** Get to the Heart of My Story*

PHENOMENAL WOMAN

A Poem by Maya Angelou

Pretty women wonder where my secret lies.
I'm not cute or built to suit a fashion model's size
But when I start to tell them,
They think I'm telling lies.
I say,
It's in the reach of my arms
The span of my hips,
The stride of my step,
The curl of my lips.
I'm a woman
Phenomenally.
Phenomenal woman,
That's me.

I walk into a room
Just as cool as you please,
And to a man,
The fellows stand or
Fall down on their knees.
Then they swarm around me,
A hive of honey bees.
I say,
It's the fire in my eyes,
And the flash of my teeth,
The swing in my waist,
And the joy in my feet.
I'm a woman
Phenomenally.
Phenomenal woman,
That's me.

Men themselves have wondered
What they see in me.
They try so much
But they can't touch
My inner mystery.
When I try to show them
They say they still can't see.
I say,
It's in the arch of my back,
The sun of my smile,
The ride of my breasts,
The grace of my style.
I'm a woman

Phenomenally.
Phenomenal woman,
That's me.

Now you understand
Just why my head's not bowed.
I don't shout or jump about
Or have to talk real loud.
When you see me passing
It ought to make you proud.
I say,
It's in the click of my heels,
The bend of my hair,
the palm of my hand,
The need of my care,
'Cause I'm a woman
Phenomenally.
Phenomenal woman,
That's me.

Chapters

Talk Show Host

MEREDITH VIEIRA

Meredith Vieira has spent most of her life as a television reporter and talk show host. She currently co-hosts the Today Show, *the most-watched morning news show in America. Prior to that, she co-hosted* The View, *another popular daytime talk show and brainchild of Barbara Walters. In addition, she has hosted the wildly successful game show,* Who Wants to Be a Millionaire, *the first show in history to award a million dollars to a contestant.*

But it was during her time as a reporter for the news magazine show, 60 Minutes, *that she became the poster child of "Can we or can't we?"—can a woman have it all, career and family? Vieira spoke and acted with conviction on this issue, thereby risking her very reputation.*

Her husband, Richard Cohen, and their three children, Ben, Gabe and Lily, have had a profound influence on her career, not only in support, but also with advice.

The Way I See It...

The nicest thing you can say about me is I am a decent person. I am real. It is important to find the real you, your real essence. Everyone will tell you who you are or what you should be. Believe in yourself and have the conviction to follow your heart.

Find your inner voice, honor that voice, and follow that voice when nobody else wants to hear it.

Family First

My mom was a tough lady and my dad was a rock. As for me, I was one of those little girls who idolize their father. Only when I was older did I appreciate my mom as a role model. I would talk to her about being a nurse since my father was a doctor, and she would tell me if I wanted to go into that field, I needed to be a doctor. I had three older brothers and my mom felt I was as good as they were, and even better.

My mom had spunk. Once, she took on the bishop in our community because she thought he was annoying and the church was sexist. My First Communion, all I wanted to do was get the host and go, but she was angry with him. So she sewed these blue flowers on my white dress...it was her way of putting up her middle finger at the bishop and saying you are not the boss of me. I was praying God didn't strike me down!

Also, I think she was a feminist. She wanted so much from me. I don't want to say she pushed me into a career, but she definitely wanted me out there in the world to make a difference. When I eventually gave up career opportunities for my family, it was hard for my mother to wrap her head around that thought. But, I know now that it worried her and she was afraid I would regret it. As time went by, she totally understood.

When I first started in television in Providence, Rhode Island, I came home crying one day because I was told I was too slow and I wouldn't make it in television news. My dad told me a lot of people are going to tell me I don't have what it takes and unless I believe in myself, I will always be taking three steps back. I went back and confronted my boss and told him I didn't care what he said. I was going to make it in this business. He just said okay, you can come back!

My father was always comfortable in his own shoes and he instilled that in his children…that faith will come from within and everything else will take care of itself.

Over the years, timing has played an important role in my career. I am not going to lie…there were economic reasons as well. I always felt it was important that I brought home a salary. That means a lot to me. My dad was "save, save, save" and I am too. I never knew when the floor might drop out from under my feet and I would be bankrupt!!

Working for *60 Minutes* was the easiest decision I have ever made. There was a lot of build-up to it. It was the only job I really, really wanted in the business. It was the best TV news magazine, without a doubt. It was 1989. I was pregnant with my son, Ben, and it was the Friday before I was to give birth by C-Section. They brought me into a meeting and offered me the job. I really didn't know what to tell them, so the president of CBS News said, "You just go home and think about it, but we'd love you to come back after having the baby to start this new job." Here I was, about to have a child and I didn't know how my life would change. But I knew it was going to change permanently. Then to be offered the best job in my business? I kept going back and forth, torn. Finally, I convinced myself I could do this. I can juggle this. I'll be a better reporter for it. I can be a better mother for it.

Soon after I started, I realized what a struggle it was going to be. I just had that feeling from Don Hewitt, the executive producer of the show. Even though he was supportive, he didn't seem to get it. I don't know if he didn't get it or if he thought I would just fit in once I got there. And the whole baby thing would just compartmentalize a little bit. I could still be part of the club. I tried to be, but I just never felt comfortable. I loved the people and worked very hard, but the culture was hard for me. I felt guilty. I wasn't with my son and family. There was always tension with Don and me. It began under the surface and then became apparent to everyone else too.

When he moved my office next to his, I knew the die was cast. The beginning of my end was my pregnancy with Gabe, my second child. I didn't tell anyone but a small circle. I told them I had a history of miscarriage so the doctor said I couldn't get on planes. Everything was just a train ride away so I wasn't worried. I hadn't told Don because I knew that would be a big deal and besides, why say anything until I was through that initial 12-week period? The likelihood that I was going to be able to carry the baby was in question.

Don called on a Saturday morning around 8:30. Richard and I were still in bed. Don was in Europe, a story had broken, and he wanted me on the Concorde to Paris. I froze. I told him I couldn't go. He said, "What?" As if whatever it is, "I'll fix it so you can get on the plane." I told him I was pregnant. I knew that would be it.

He followed that up with wanting me to go to a toxic waste dump in Russia. I called Al Gore who was involved in it and he said I shouldn't get near the place. I called Don and told him I couldn't do it.

Near the end, I said to Don, "I'm going to take my six month maternity leave as a part time employee, so there is no way I can do 20 stories. I am already doing 10 stories and it is impossible because I am not going to be here."

He said, "It is that or nothing." I didn't lose any sleep that night. It was very clear if I had to choose one over the other, I was going to go with my personal life…I was going to go with my family. To not do that would be such a disaster for me on every level.

At the time, it was big news. Right after I made the decision to leave *60 Minutes*, Richard and I attended an event and a woman confronted me. "You can't leave *60 Minutes*! Your leaving suggests to women that we can't have it all. It sends the wrong message." She was offended.

I was firm in my conviction. "No, my staying when I feel it is wrong sends the wrong message."

Everyone has to make up their own mind about what is right for them. I don't think you can have it all. Life is about setting your priorities…making decisions…and not just assuming that anything you can *put* on that plate, you can *have* on that plate. It is about balance and choices. I wanted to exceed at the experiment of having a family and having a job I always coveted. I think the decision to leave was the right one, but you always wonder, "What if I had played the political game more?"

I never missed an interview opportunity to say, "My life is my family." I'm sure Don would hear that and say, *"Shut up; family—shamily*!" It felt like a smear campaign after I left the show. Don was quoted in the paper. "Whoever heard of the Meredith Vieira story anyway?" It was very vicious that he went after my professional life. No one had ever questioned that before. I felt it was a real cheap shot, below the belt. Go after me in any way you want, but don't go after my work. He made these statements just to take away from the notion that "Don took a job away from a pregnant lady." And that wasn't fair either. That was bologna. He had women at the show sign a letter saying I was not doing my fair share, having babies and not working as hard as men. I was very hurt and angry, but not at the women. There was just a lot of pressure in that place. Some people felt that way and that was okay, but I know my assistant felt pressured and refused to sign it and she suffered for that. He strong-armed people. Pitting women against each other is wrong.

Now, of course, they are much more flexible in this business. I will always regret the pain that Richard and I were put through

My next venture was to anchor the CBS Early, Early News. I didn't know if it was the right spot for me, but it was all they had. I had to have a job. I think to this day, that is why I got pregnant again so soon after I took the job at *60 Minutes*. I may have felt like I failed because that is my M.O., so I don't like to attach too much significance to it. I am one of those people who think they are not good enough. I don't know why because I received nothing but positive reinforcement as a kid. I beat up on myself a bit. Insecure…the banana peel is right around the corner!

I later moved to ABC News hoping for a better feeling about work, family, and myself. And I found it there. When I had Lily, my third and last child, things were working great until they told me I would have to start doing *20/20* and *Primetime* stories, along with my regular job. I said to them, "Why would I leave *60 Minutes* to come and do the same amount of work here?"

That is when *The View* opportunity came up. The producer's biggest concern—was I funny enough. Someone said I was crazy, but they didn't know if I was funny! I didn't want to do it at first, I pooh-poohed the idea. But Richard sat me down. "Go do it…you are a reporter that doesn't want to report and that is sort of a dead end, don't you think?" Then he gave me one of his looks.

I came home after the audition embarrassed, thinking I have 20 years in the news business and now I am thinking about a talk show. Excuse me for thinking I was some big deal, but I didn't really watch morning television. I thought it could be fun, but there was no way they would hire me anyway.

But, then they did! And I loved the show. I loved the people and many of my friends are still there. I worked on *The View* for nine years when I was asked to do the *Today Show*. What a surprise! My whole career has been a surprise. I was surprised when Jeff Zucker, head of NBC, asked me to host the *Today Show* at 52 years old. I jokingly told him he was skewing a little old for this job. He told me he was looking for experience. Joking again, I said, "You could have said I'm not old!"

It may be unfair to say this is a young people's business, especially when it comes to women. I look around and I see Diane Sawyer at *Good Morning America*, and she is older than I am and looks fantastic. Nobody would question her credentials or say she is getting a little long in the tooth. I think it is great that my offer came from a man too. The show was in a predicament of sorts, losing Katie Couric after 15 years. She is an icon in the business. I think they checked out the landscape and they thought, wait a minute, this person actually has the skill set we need...news and entertainment.

While considering their offer, I was in a fetal position for several months in my home, crying. I carried the list of why I should take the job and why I shouldn't in my coat pocket all the time, afraid I was going to throw it out. I had a cushy job with *The View*. I could almost do it with my eyes closed. I had another job with *Who Wants to Be a Millionaire* on top of that. Why would I want to switch this life? Do I really want to go back to news? Oh, I would just cry.

Richard thought it was a no-brainer. He said I came home saying I was bored and I was too young to be bored. The children played a part in the decision too. They had all asked me to stop talking about them on *The View*. That is what you do on the show—you talk about your life. For that reason, it was time for me to think of doing something else because I needed to stop talking about them! Unless I became a jet setter and started talking about my wild partying, it wasn't going to change. My middle child provided the greatest contribution to the decision. I said, "I'm not going to be here for you at breakfast," and he said, "What are you going to miss? We fight."

I had fear of failure, taking over after Katie. Scary! Fear of success too. What if this works? Then I am stuck.

That is the difference between men and women: a man never says I am scared of success. It could be a gender thing or a conditioned thing because they are taught to go out there and be a success and win, a macho thing.

Eventually, I decided to stretch myself and do it since it could be the last traditional job I would ever have because I would be dead at the end of it! The night before the first show, Richard and the kids gave me a gold bracelet that is all scratched up now because I never take it off. It says *We are with you. Love, Richard, Ben, Gabe and Lily.*

"'Stay' is a charming word in a friend's vocabulary."

—Louisa May Alcott
(1832–1888) American writer

JOANNE CARSON

Joanne Carson is best known as the former wife of Johnny Carson, the legendary Tonight Show *host and television entertainer. Her life and career cross several paths, including airline stewardess, actress, model and teacher. She hosted her own talk show called* Joanne Carson's VIP's *in the 1970s.*

Earning her Ph.D. in Psychology in 1981, she parlayed her television credentials into a job as host of another television show called Alive and Well.

Believing that "dogs and cats are the only creatures on God's earth that are totally accepting," she helped start Actors and Others for Animals *in 1971 to further the public's understanding of the plight of animals.*

The amazing Howard Hughes was a good friend to Carson, but her roommate and best friend in life was Truman Capote.

Joanne, now in her seventies, lives in Beverly Hills, California and has recently adopted a retired racing greyhound, all of 4 years old.

The Way I See It...

When you see a door open, if you don't step forward, you will miss it. You have to step toward a closed door and it will open for you. If you stop and wait for it to open, it won't.

Living a Purposeful Life

I was abandoned at the age of six months and left in a convent. Not a very charmed life, but I like to say it was a purposeful one. I had what I call a reversed childhood. My mother gave birth to me and proudly handed me over to my father.

My mother was a successful top female athlete. She played golf, but started in tennis. Bobby Riggs would only play tennis with a few chosen people—she was one of them. She was an extremely bright lady.

Since it was the depression, my lawyer father was out of a job. So for the first six months of my life while my mother went to work, my father raised me...and then they divorced. After the divorce, I lived with the next door neighbors, but after the man died, the wife could no longer care for me. So, the Convent of San Louis Ray took me in.

If nothing else, my mother taught me independence. Emotionally, she removed herself from me and other people. I was on my own and had to learn at a very young age how to be acceptable, polite and liked—*really* liked.

Mischievous and bored, I put sugar in the salt shakers and salt in the sugar bowls at the convent. I had housemaid's knees covered in calluses, forever on my knees praying for my sins. The regimented life comforted me though. I didn't like it, but I knew it was teaching me something. I believe my father's deep love for me while he cared for me every day as a baby made me instinctively prepared to live with the nuns.

I remember Dudley Moore, the actor, once told me that when he was very young, he was hospitalized with a club foot deformity. One of the nurses gave him a kiss on the forehead and he never forgot the way that kiss felt. He said that "going toward good feelings" made him successful.

That is what I did in the convent. I remember times when I would be sitting in the convent foyer with my suitcase waiting for my parents... all the girls would be leaving...and 5:00 would come, and one of the nuns would have to take me back to my room. But I always instinctively reached for good thoughts and creative outlets.

Finally, my father decided that if I stayed at the convent any longer, I would become one of the nuns. He remarried to give me a home.

My father gave me such wisdom. One day, in answer to my question, "How am I supposed to live in this world?" he told me to look in the street gutter and then up to the sky. He said not to look down, but to remember what was in the gutter. He said that is like life...you know what is in the gutter and you don't have to look there. If you have a choice in life, look only to the beautiful things. That was my first step to positive thinking.

Another time, I asked him, "How do I get to be a beautiful, grown-up lady?" He looked at me knowingly and said, "Joanne, everyone you meet in life will take away a part of you and you will take away a part of them...but it is the part of people that they offer in love that will make you a grown-up lady." I took that advice to heart, so I went from shy to outgoing, wanting to meet everybody for the gift they were going to give me!

My stepmother never liked me. She finally told my father, "She's got to go." Rebellious, I just ran away and was homeless at 15, but only for about three nights. I was sleeping in Plummer Park and I met a lady who brought me sandwiches and told me I could work as a Mother's Helper for $5 a week plus room and board. She gave me a newspaper with the ads in it. I hopped on the bus and went to one of the houses in the paper.

When the woman answered the door, she announced that she wasn't interviewing because it was Saturday. I looked past her and saw a television set! This was 1948...people didn't have television sets. Her husband sold televisions and I knew I had to live in that house! I looked her straight in the eye and told her, "That's okay...I'll take the job." I walked right in and asked where my room was. If you don't know the rules, you just make them up to work for you. She was so taken back by this that she gave me a strange look and said, "Oh." She showed me the room. Her name was Alice Davidson, and she became quite a mentor to me.

While working as a mother's helper, I returned to school. My grades had been horrible while living with my stepmother. Now, suddenly, they turned around.

After I finished high school, my father wanted me to go to college. In the 1950s, girls just wanted to have fun. We didn't have any serious expectations. Fathers thought girls would go to college, have fun and get married. It was expected of me. So I went to a liberal arts college but didn't finish.

I wanted to be a stewardess—it seemed so exotic—I wanted to fly all over the world. I decided to interview with Pan Am, even though they only hired about three people a year. They had an open call with 536 girls for three spots. Some even had nursing training. But I didn't care. I just wanted to fly. I made the first cut. They were down to 100 girls. I didn't have the credentials so I made up things…two years of college (But I know I can fly!), 21 years old (I will be if you hire me!), nurses training (I took Red Cross!). When they said you don't have another language, I said take me to the terminal to talk to people from other countries. Sure enough, I figured out how to help them without knowing their language. They said, "Joanne, you're not 5'5". So I put lifts inside my stockings during a lunch break and put my shoes back on. When the head stewardess measured me, she said, "I don't know how you managed to grow two inches, but if you want to be a stewardess that bad, you are hired."

On one of the military air transport flights to Wake Island, I met a civilian named Mr. Howard who was a drinker. He looked a little shaky with a day's growth of beard and shoes with no socks. I thought, "This poor guy!"

I was reading a book about Tyrone Power and Mr. Howard leaned over and asked, "Is that a good book?" We started talking about movies and how much I wanted to be an actress and how Katherine Hepburn was our favorite actress. When we got to Wake, he said he would love to help me with a movie career.

Jokingly I said, "I'm sorry, Mr. Howard, but you have to have a movie studio to help me." We parted and I headed for the beach. While sunning, I looked up and in the distance, here he comes, pale as a white shirt. I offered to put lotion on him so he wouldn't burn to a crisp. He asked me to pose for a photo to get the Coral Reef background. The water matched my turquoise bathing suit so I posed for the picture.

A couple of hours later, he left. I continued on my flight to Japan and came home. The guy at the flight desk called me over and said, "A guy who works for RKO Studio wants to talk to you about a contract."

I said, "Yeah, right."

He kept calling and finally I met with him. He told me, "Howard Hughes is very interested in putting you under contract."

I said, "Who is he? I've never met anyone named Howard Hughes." He showed me the picture from the beach! I told him, "That's Mr. Hughes? I thought his name was Mr. Howard. He *owns* TWA?"

I knew nothing about contracts, so I told the man from RKO that he needed to talk to my father. When my father met Howard, he discovered that they were born on the same day one year apart. Suddenly, Mr. Hughes lost the image of a lecherous producer with a stable of girlfriends. My father looked at Howard as a man who would look after me. I signed the contract.

When I arrived in Los Angeles, they picked me up every morning in a limo, did my hair and clothes, took publicity stills and sent me to acting classes. I was not happy. I didn't know that being an actress would be like this. I told them, "I quit." The manager laughed...looked at me in shock...ignored my remark...took a step forward and pointed his finger at my face and said, "You can't leave...you are under contract and you'll be outlawed from all the other studios too!"

I told him, "Fine, I don't want to work for any other studio."

He called Howard and I met with him at the Paul Hessey Studio. I had a bone to pick with him. I found it rude that he hadn't told me who he really was.

He made me feel very foolish. He explained that it was his habit to be secretive about who he was and where he was.

I told him why I wanted to quit the studio. I thought acting was when you were given a story and you said whatever you wanted to say to the camera. I couldn't remember lines and say somebody else's words. Then I told him acting was too slow...you stood around too much, not moving.

He gave me some valuable advice. He told me I didn't need to be lit and screened and retouched. My best bet was television because I was a direct person. He said he would make some calls and fly me to New York to see how I liked it.

I was 21 and had no idea how fortunate I was. I asked him why he was going to such trouble for me. He smiled, "You have a mind that moves on ball bearings."

We became very good friends. We stayed in touch. He gave me a number in Los Angeles if I ever needed to get in touch with him and they would connect me to wherever he was. I really had a great friend in Howard. He flew me to New York and made arrangements for me with an agency and I was on to my next life.

Howard Hughes would call me often and ask, "Are you enjoying the world of modeling?"

I replied, "No, because I am not tall enough to be a runway model."

He said again, "Joanne, why don't you try television commercials?" So I took his advice, and did try television commercials along with doing some commercial modeling. Then I worked my way up from a model who handed out prizes like Vanna White to a job on the *Today Show* with Dave Garroway. I co-hosted a game show in 1960 called *Video Village* that was also shown on Friday nights on CBS. My achievements amazed me!

In 1960, my dad called me to have dinner…with a wonderful guy named Johnny Carson. I said, "Who the hell is that?"

He says, "He has a day time game show on ABC."

To which I reply, "He's not in my league!"

Then my dad says, "I've already invited him!" So I agreed to the dinner.

As soon as Johnny introduced himself and smiled, the sun came out. I was instantly and absolutely enchanted.

He was a man who wouldn't compromise his thoughts. When my father wanted him to hear my sister play the violin to get his advice about sending her to Juilliard, Johnny looked at him straight in the eye and said, "Mr. Copeland, save your money." That was when I knew I was going to marry him…a man after my own heart.

Johnny was 35 and I was 28. He had just come out of a very unsettling marriage and I had no intentions of marrying. He invited me over to his apartment the next night to see a comedy show. I made a joke about this being the new line to get a woman in your apartment and he turned bright red and got redder and redder. He was very sensitive. We had dinner 10 nights in a row.

As a new bachelor, his apartment was bare…one couch, one table, one lamp, and not even a coffee table. I would bring over stuff to fill out this very bare apartment and one day, three or four months later, I brought my ironing board and he said very calmly, "Why do I get the feeling you have just moved in on me?" By this time, everything of mine was at his apartment and bringing the ironing board meant *this was it*. I had to iron my outfits for the next day's show.

The admiration I had for him as a talent, as a person, as a very shy, sweet person overcame my resistance to marriage.

In 1962, we made the decision about the *Tonight Show*. We were partners. We discussed what kind of show he wanted to do and what imprint he wanted to put on it. For the next 10 years, the show was in New York because Johnny didn't like Los Angeles.

Unfortunately, I became ill and the doctors didn't know how to diagnose me. I felt worse and worse living in New York. I knew I had to get back to Los Angeles. New York society was deadly...caste-oriented...where is your brownstone...your weekend house...who are your friends. All status, status, status. The apartment we lived in on the river in the UN Plaza was very status, so I couldn't go to the lobby with sneakers and a ponytail.

As much as I loved Johnny, I was dealing with doctors who kept giving me valium or ritalin which only made me worse. I was at a point of desperation. I had to get back to Los Angeles. I also had to leave Johnny, the man I loved, to find me again. I really felt Johnny did not need me anymore.

Johnny wasn't happy about me moving back home, but he didn't want another marriage breaking up. We did drift apart during our two years of a long distance relationship. Johnny was angry with me. He would say, "Joanne, you belong with me and should support how I make a living."

Sadly, I said to him, "I cannot be me any longer in this stifling environment in New York." I know Johnny didn't understand me or my feelings at that time. I realize now I hurt him deeply. Not angry in the way that he would never speak to me, but he was hurt. You see, the Johnny that I had known early on needed me. I was able to leave him because I felt he was pretty much established and didn't really need me anymore. I remember telling him," I don't have a talent, but I care about you and I always have." His kids were in high school and I felt I needed to get on with my life.

I moved back to California and I was correctly diagnosed with hypoglycemia, a deadly thing to be dealing with when you don't know what it is. My emotions were all over the place. One minute, I was laughing and the next, I was crying. I was depressed and then on top of the world. It was a yo-yo period for me. I was determined to find me again, and I knew I could in Los Angeles.

There has always been something out there for me to do...always more to do. I believe everything has a life span...friendships and marriages. When you complete it, you should move on and if you stay and don't grow then they should plant you somewhere else. You need to keep moving on.

I cared deeply about Johnny and loved him from the minute I met him and never stopped loving him, but he was in New York and I had to live in California. It was important for Johnny and me to remain friends. We worked at our friendship in our own private war.

Opportunities float around people all day long, but they are like little doors that open for a few seconds and then close. If you are a bright person, then you move quickly. If you don't step forward when you see a door open, you will miss it. If you stop and wait for it to open, it won't.

I met Truman Capote in 1966 at a dinner party. We bonded immediately because we were both abandoned as children, he to relatives and I to the convent. As Truman said, we were joined at the hip from there on up. We spoke every day. He tried to talk me out of moving back to California. He said, "You have all these perks….a great position…you're married to one of the most powerful men in the country…you can pick up the phone and call the White House…unlimited access to money…what more could you want?"

I replied, "I want to go home. I need to go home." My illness was undiagnosed—no one understood that I needed to be home. I told Truman, "I feel Los Angeles is where I need to be at this time in my life."

Truman finally understood, "Okay then… I will find you a house in Los Angeles." He moved in with me. I wanted a two bedroom cottage. He picked a five bedroom house so he could have three bedrooms to himself. He explained, "Joanne, I like to have space to create."

I told him, "Fine," because he was my advisor and my true friend. We understood each other. He became my everything.

As life continued forward, and about two years later, Johnny met someone and wanted to get married. It was a difficult period, because Johnny and I had pure love. Truman Capote stood by and would say, "Joanne, you amaze me." I knew Truman adored and appreciated me. He helped me realize what all the men in my life had really meant to me.

Once Truman and I were settled, I decided to walk through yet another door of opportunity. I went back into television. I realized the demographics were going to be against me and I needed to change my course. In the 1970s, when you were 40, that was like being 70 today. It was a syndicated show called *Joanne Carson's VIP's*. I had a guest, Adele Davis, who had written a book about nutrition and health. The topic fascinated me. I bought all her books. I started going to seminars and eventually got my Masters in Psychology and my Ph.D. I knew there was a body-mind connection. At that time, nutrition was not considered a field of study and no graduate degree existed. I immersed myself in the field anyway.

In 1984, my world turned upside down. Truman died and I lost my balance. Truman was the great love and friend of my life. He was 59 and had a double addiction to drugs and alcohol that he fought tooth and nail. Where I had gone into the health field to get better, he went the other way. He came to me when he was dying; he knew something was very wrong. He flew in on Thursday and died Saturday morning. I wanted to call the paramedics and he said, "If you love me, please don't. No more hospitals. No more doctors. I can't do this anymore." I just held him. His last word was "Mother." He never gained her favor, ever spending his life trying.

Truman's death hit me hard. My father died at 59 also. My mother was deceased too. I felt abandoned again even though all my life I had turned rejection into a heartfelt experience.

The loss of Truman was too great, I went underground. I left television. I didn't want to be observed anymore. I lost that sparkle. I was 52 and thought "I have survived a half century. I could rest on my laurels."

Thank goodness Johnny and I were still good friends…he was there when I lost Truman and I was there when he lost his son, Ricky. A private friendship helped us both in times of need.

The key in my life has been the *caring gene*, my motherly instinct that allowed me to share special gifts with others. At a very young age, I chose not to have children. I realized that I was much too selfish to raise a child. I had to raise myself first.

Now, we live in an age when it is okay for women to have careers and not be married and have their own life. I say you have to be selfish to do this and people don't understand that.

My mother was a very strong woman, a very independent woman, a great role model for me. The women and men in my life have all been very bright, but I don't think intelligence is a criterion for a woman. I believe that nurturing is more important than intelligence, because all the book learning in the world is not going to help if you don't have an instinct to nurture and allow it.

I see myself more as a facilitator. My nurturing instinct knows how to be supportive of people, genuinely supportive. I could get out of my own way when dealing with other people—my feelings and my needs have never been in my way.

I now work with AIDS patients and my Catholic background has made it very hard to let go of people. I learned this life is very temporary because it is preparing us to evolve to help mankind. We are here for a purpose, a reason. Many people miss the opportunity of evolving and furthering mankind. They don't live a purposeful life. And just because you find that purpose, it doesn't mean that is the end of it. There are other stages of growth. I learned about success and power, yet these things in my life came with personal sacrifice.

I am excited. Every day is a new day, with new opportunities of discovery for me. I keep learning and meeting people, evolving. There is wonderful movement in my life.

Sports

"The way I see it, if you want the rainbow, you gotta put up with the rain."

—Dolly Parton
American singer & actress

ANNE ABERNATHY

Anne Abernathy is the oldest woman to ever compete in the Olympics, winter or summer. She started in sports when most people retire, and her trek as an Olympic Luge athlete lasted 26 years. Along the way, she battled cancer three times and suffered a head injury, multiple broken bones, 15 knee surgeries and a broken back.

Abernathy was given the nickname "Grandma Luge" by the German Luge Team in 1993 when she was 40 years old. At that time, luge athletes were expected to retire from the sport at the age of 30. She never thought of age as a barrier.

She is in her fifties now, making appearances and speaking publicly about her experiences, as well as developing a TV and radio series.

In addition, she realizes it is time for her to be a mentor and a coach.

The Way I See It...

Step up, not back. When someone says you *cannot*, say *why not* and just do it.

Why Not Just Do It?

I had no idea I was going to be an Olympic athlete.

When I was growing up, women were not even supposed to *do* sports. My mother was from the South and there was no way her daughter was going to be in sports—maybe swimming and tennis because they were "feminine" sports. Swimming was fine with me, since I am from St. Thomas in the Caribbean, but I also wanted to play softball and do other sports in school.

After college, snow skiing caught my attention, so my parents gave me a ski trip for Christmas. I went with a group of friends to Lake Placid, New York and the ski conditions were absolutely horrible. Ice everywhere. Someone suggested we watch the bobsled training. Because the Olympic/Winter Games had taken place in Lake Placid in 1980, everyone knew what bobsled was.

We watched a bobsled come down the track with four men in it slamming the walls, left and right. They had on shoulder pads and helmets and were holding their heads between their knees. I thought…this can't be fun…these men are nuts, absolutely nuts!

I saw a sign pointing to the luge track and thought…what the heck is luge? Just as we walked up, a sled went flying by at an incredible speed. After watching the noisy bobsleds banging down the track, the luge seemed to float by. How cool! About 20 of us gathered beside the track. A luge coach standing up on the track wall asked anyone who wanted to try it to take a step forward. Immediately, 18 people took a step back and there I was, still standing in front, and I thought, why not?

That started the journey. Luge became my passion. After my first run down the track I was hooked. I totally loved to luge. It wasn't that I wanted to go to the Olympics. The Virgin Islands, my home, had never had a Winter Olympic team, so competing in the Olympics did not even appear to be a possibility.

Not without a struggle, it happened. In 1988, I became a member of the first Virgin Islands Winter Olympic Team! However, two years before the Olympics, I was told not to train because I probably wouldn't live that long. I was diagnosed with cancer. One of my doctors told me to focus on getting well. I replied, "My job is to get to the Olympics; your job is to get me well!" From that point on, my medical team viewed me as the "Olympic Hopeful," not the cancer victim. They even nicknamed me "Annemule" because I was so stubborn in my conviction and focus.

Perseverance paid off when the cancer went into remission. I qualified for my first Olympics in Calgary, but a new obstacle presented itself: age discrimination.

You weren't supposed to luge after the age of 30, but no one had told me. On the German team if you were 30, you had to retire. The day before the competition, as we were going down the track, the announcers were practicing what they were going to say about the athletes, in German, French and English. I finished one run and returned back up to the top where my coach from Austria and a German athlete were looking at me and laughing. My coach told me the announcers were saying I was 33 years old. I told him I *was* 33 and he said, "No, your German is not so good...you are 23."

I stood there calmly. "Your English isn't so good and I am 33!"

He looked at me incredulously. "You can't be 33...I am only 32 and I am retired."

I held my ground. "That's your problem, not mine."

The German athlete started laughing, stood up and put his hands on his hips and said, "Anne, you are too old to luge."

I stared at him. "I wasn't five minutes ago!"

Five Olympics later in the 2002 Salt Lake City Games, that same German athlete came up to me and said he owed me a beer. I looked him straight in the eye. "The entire German women's luge team owes me a keg!" He had just won his fifth Olympic medal and the German women's team had swept the luge medals, yet they were all older than I was in my first Olympics when I was declared "too old to luge."

Without realizing it, I opened a barrier for these Olympic medalists who would have been passed by because someone picked an arbitrary retirement age of 30 to signify an athlete was too old to compete. My first Olympics, I was 33 and the oldest luge athlete, male or female that year, and every year after that...and now I have been in six Olympics. When the German athlete told me I should not luge, my response automatically was, "Why not?"

My struggles continued. One of the most difficult things I went through was my recovery from a 2001 crash in Altenberg, Germany. During a World Cup race I had a devastating crash. The live telecast waited for 20 minutes for the rescue team to climb into the icy track to recover my limp body. When I woke up, I had lost three years of memory and didn't recognize my roommate and medical coach, Melita Glanville. The head injury was severe, causing blackouts, seizures, and impaired balance. A conventional doctor told me that I would probably never drive a car again much less compete in the Salt Lake City Olympics less than a year away. I was determined to find a way.

I relocated to California to undergo brain biofeedback therapy which basically meant playing video games with your brain—no joystick, just wires connected to your head. Neither Melita, who was monitoring me 24/7, or my new doctor ever let on that they had any doubts about my recovery. My doctor's only promise to me was that he would work as hard as I did.

It was all I could do to get back on the race circuit, much less qualify. In fact, the first time I put my sled on the luge track after my crash, I thought for a moment, "Am I nuts?" Then the green track light went on. I lay on the sled and, like riding a bike, I went right into it again. I can only imagine the trepidation everyone else had.

It was definitely a team effort, and together we broke the medical "barrier" that many said would keep me from Olympic competition. Instead of saying, "cannot," we focused on "why not."

Just four weeks before the 2002 Salt Lake City Olympic Opening Ceremony, I qualified for my fifth Olympics. I was the last person to qualify but I did it. Still, the possibility of finishing last in the race hit me and my self esteem sank. What was I doing here? Then I saw an Olympic kiosk where the fact of the day stated that Anne Abernathy was to be the oldest woman to ever compete in the Olympics. I was making history and hadn't even realized it. Signs everywhere cheered me on. I realized then that it wasn't important where I finished. The important thing was that I was there. I had overcome—and broken yet another barrier—setting a new Olympic record in the process. I had already won because I was there.

Setting my sights on the 2006 Olympics in Torino, Italy was a difficult decision. It would be a tough road both physically and financially. Aside from that, I was already in the record books, so I wasn't sure what I wanted to accomplish.

While pondering the decision, I was invited to speak at a Red Hat Society Convention, a social group primarily for women over the age of

50 who, aside from wearing red hats, congregate to have fun. During my speech, I told the audience that if I did compete in the upcoming Olympics, I would have to wear this…and I pulled out a red helmet! There was an immediate standing ovation. Following my talk, I was surrounded by women that wanted to help me reach my sixth competition. My motto was "Slide for Six in 2006!" Returning home, a message on my answering machine from a woman who had heard my speech simply said, "What do we have to do to get your butt to the Olympics?"

I was in the unique position to be the first woman over 50 to qualify for the Winter Olympic Games and these women wanted someone to represent them. Breaking the 50 year age barrier was even more important than the 30 year age mark, and I would soon find out, an even more daunting task. Although I represented the U.S. Virgin Islands in the Olympics, these women over the age of 50 became my *nation*. They provided the impetus for me to train for four more hard years.

Leading up to the Torino Winter Olympic Games was a big build-up in the international media and press, including an *NBC Nightly News* feature showing me carrying the flag in the opening ceremony. What an emotional experience. This race would be the end of an era: six Olympics, 283 international races, three decades, the oldest woman, the first over 50, a 37 year difference between the oldest and the youngest in an event. The next oldest athlete in women's luge was 17 years younger than me.

Everything was going great. My training times were getting faster with each run. My goal to set my personal best finish and time during the race was on track.

Then, I crashed.

The crash broke my wrist and the scapula in my back, but more than that, it broke my heart. The news was broadcast everywhere. Within the first 12 hours I received over 1,600 e-mails from around the world. I was afraid to read them…afraid they would call me a loser, afraid that I had let everyone down. Instead I was amazed to read the level of support and encouragement from complete strangers. Their uplifting messages enabled me to view my "agony of defeat" in an entirely different way.

Although extremely painful both physically and emotionally, I'm not sure my sports career would have been complete without the Olympic crash. I have experienced the extreme highs as well as the lows of the Olympic journey. By doing so, I have a clearer understanding of how to relate to individuals no matter where they are on this roller coaster called life.

Many people dream of being at the Olympics…I was there not once, not twice, but six times and despite the mishaps and crashes I wouldn't change it for anything in the world. I was able to do something that I truly loved and learned about life as well.

I tell people looking for a purpose, "When you see anything that catches your eye, try it. Don't step back, step up." If I had taken a step back when the luge coach offered us a chance to ride, I would not be telling you this story.

If an opportunity sets itself in front of you, be bold enough to accept it. Then if you enjoy it, run out and do everything you can to follow that passion. You never know where it may lead. Remember there are no age limits on dreams. I didn't find my passion for luge until I was 30.

"Aerodynamically the bumblebee shouldn't be able to fly,
but the bumblebee doesn't know that, so it goes on flying anyway."

—*Mary Kay Ash*
(1918–2001) American businesswoman

DIANE CRUMP

Diane Crump, the first female jockey to run in the Kentucky Derby is also the first female to ride in a pari-mutuel race in the United States. A thrilling career as a jockey and horsewoman fulfilled her every dream.

Now, she lives in Virginia, putting her extensive knowledge and experience to work in equine sales.

The Way I See It...

The main thing is I completed the job.

A Leg Up

At four years old, I rode my first pony at a carnival. From that second forward, I was smitten by the horse bug. It was *in me*. I drew horse heads on everything.

Driven to have my own horse, I worked and saved every cent. In the summer, I would paint people's furniture, clean, deliver newspapers, whatever it took. I put up posters for jobs at feed and tack stores. I started a riding club. By the time I was 12, I had saved $140, enough for a horse.

One day while riding my horse, I noticed a road called Race Track Road that led into a horse track. All of a sudden, the fascination to ride on that track hit me just like my first pony ride. I was possessed. I rode my horse every day until I could find a way to get in and gallop around that track.

My first real job at age 13 was on a Florida race horse farm owned by an Italian man who loved racing. I convinced him to smuggle me in to the local race track…kids under 16 weren't allowed. He introduced me to a trainer and I started washing water buckets and cleaning stalls, thrilled to be there. There were no women around, but since I was just a kid, everyone was friendly to me. I blended in. I started riding the horses. I learned to gallop…and reached the point where I was pretty decent. But as time went by, I wanted to *ride in a race.* It had never been a real possibility for any woman. Only men rode races.

All the women riders wanted to ride, not just gallop. Since I had been galloping horses for several years, I was certainly competent to ride. I found out that Olympic rider Kathy Kushner had taken legal action because the race track officials wouldn't allow her to ride in pari-mutuel races. A group of women lawyers donated their time and effort to her fight because they felt *they* had been discriminated against in the law profession. They thought it was horrible that Kathy could ride in the Olympics but not in a race. Her lawyers, through the court of Maryland, won her the right to race.

As soon as I heard the results of the case, I decided to go for a license. I had never thought it possible. I applied at Churchhill Downs racetrack. One other girl obtained a license too. The very last day of the meet, she was supposed to ride a race. They moved her race to the last one because everybody was up in arms about a woman riding. The trainers, the other jockeys, the fans, people on the backside, everybody thought it was insane that a woman would be allowed to ride in a race. In the end, the riders boycotted her...if *she* rode, *they* wouldn't.

Most people thought women were too weak to ride. We "couldn't handle it, couldn't control the horses." They were prejudiced. We could certainly gallop any horse that anybody else could gallop; that is almost harder than riding a race. I became an outspoken advocate for women riders, determined to prove our talent.

Since horse racing follows a circuit around the country, we left Churchhill Downs for the Hialeah racetrack. The people I worked for were serious and wanted me to ride, not just gallop and work out the horses. I was galloping one day when out of the clear blue sky, an owner's wife pointed to me and said, "This woman has tried so hard and everyone is giving her such a hassle, I want you to put her on my horse and let her ride in the race tomorrow morning." I had never heard of this couple, but they had been keeping up with the press about me and they thought I deserved the right to ride.

Trying to avoid conflict, the racetrack stewards wrote an article in the racing forum saying "if a woman is named to ride at Hialeah, we had better not have any male jockeys boycotting. The law is in place and these girls have proven that they deserve the opportunity. We will rule you off if you boycott a woman. Or you will be fined for breaking the law."

The Horsemen's Benevolent Protection Association, HBPA, put me in their office right behind the men's jock room. By rule, jockeys have to stay inside two hours before the race. When I went to the bathroom to change, the stewards told the other male riders they had to ride against me. "If you all boycott her, we will replace you with exercise riders." Lo and behold, every single rider *rode* against me! For the first time, they didn't boycott a woman. That is how I became the first woman to ride.

I had a police escort. I was a spectacle. They could hardly get me to the paddock because the people were so tight around me. They couldn't weigh me in the men's jock room because I wasn't allowed in there. They took the scales *outside* and weighed me. It was the largest crowd in the paddock at Hialeah since the Swaps national match race in the '50s. Over 65,000 people crowded around watching me basically "get my orders and get my leg up." Throngs of people—some *for* me and some *against* me—wanted to see what would happen next.

Luckily I am just one of those people that don't get upset or nervous. I didn't pay attention to anything; it all rolled off of me. I looked straight ahead, walked to the paddock, introduced myself to the trainer and shook his hand. He told me about the horse, gave me a leg up and patted my leg. "Good luck and do the best you can. You're in a tough spot." He knew my horse didn't belong in that race; the odds were 50 to 1.

Still, this was a dream. I focused on what they were telling me and the job at hand. I wanted to give the best ride that I could. My first race ever! A long hard race for my horse too, longer than usual.

It was chaotic, people calling to me and heckling me.

Just before the race, I forgot to put my goggles down and a top male rider, Craig Perret, in the gate next to me said, "Diane, put your goggles down!" I was a bit preoccupied. The next minute, they sprung the gate and we were off! I didn't feel nervous but obviously I was affected. I rode my race and finished 10th out of 12.

The press complimented my ride. "She knew what she was doing." One woman said, "Look at her, she's breathing harder than the horse." Another man said, "Yea, you try it." Comments went back and forth like that. The main thing is I completed the job.

From there, it didn't take me long to *win* my first race and become the first woman to ever win a stakes race. Only one other woman in the country, Barbara Jo Rubin, was riding at that time. Her trainer thought if she was the first girl to *win* a race, it would give them financial gain. She did that, but I was the first one to *ride*. She ended up only riding for a year. I stuck it out for 30 years.

No one really believed a woman could perform as well as a male rider. Even though it had happened, they thought it was a fluke. I ended up winning about 10 races at Gulfstream racetrack and in the meantime, was paid by Thistle Downs, Braniff Airlines and others for promotional riding.

Little by little, women were gaining acceptance on the race track. It took me almost ten years to be considered even half way equal to the male riders. For the first couple of years, the men hated us. We were a blow to their ego.

Eventually everyone realized that in this game of racing, it's hard to win no matter who you are. It takes work and perseverance. You're out there at 5 a.m., getting on as many horses as you can every morning, struggling. As a woman, I would have to gallop 20 horses to get named to one in a race. And that would be the one nobody else wanted; it would be 50 to 1. That went on for years. And it's still not equal.

The fact that I was consistent and not a smart aleck helped me. I didn't have anything bad to say. I loved what I did and worked hard every day—seven days a week, 365 days a year. I rode whatever I could. It took that steady grind to gain acceptance.

At first, women were not allowed in the barn area after 5:00 at night because men didn't think it was proper. The rules were very antiquated. As the years wore on, you would see a few more women—women grooms, women hotwalkers, women exercise riders. At one point I was probably the only woman in the country who had an exerciser's license.

After my first few months of racing, Puerto Rico wanted me to ride a match race against an old pro. I was a kid. I didn't know the ins and outs. I just knew to try.

I took my horse out of the gate and around the first turn and the backside. From the corner of my eye, I saw my opponent, this old timer, holding my saddle towel for probably a quarter of a mile, an old trick to slow you down. My horse was actually helping him along. When I realized what was happening, he moved up and knocked my foot out of the stirrup. I hit him on the hand with my stick hoping he would lose his reins. As he dropped the reins, I grabbed them, and he tried to push me off my horse. We literally fought hand and foot the whole way. He ended up beating me by a length. When we came back around to face the crowd, they started screaming and bombarding him with eggs and tomatoes. By the time he walked back to the jock's room, he was a mess.

I went to Canada to ride in a stakes race where no woman had ever ridden. They put me in a little room around the corner from the jock's room. The whole feeling was very anti-woman. At least in America, you were allowed to weigh in with lightweight boots, but the Canadian officials said I had to weigh in with my regular racing boots. They said my riding stick was two inches too long. Nobody wanted to loan me another stick. Nobody wanted to take my tack. Not one rider spoke to me and not one reporter interviewed me. It was like I didn't exist. Nothing.

My filly was favored at number three in the race, but after her long road trip up there, she wasn't her normal self. By the eighth pole, two of the riders pinned me so tightly I couldn't even pick up my stick. I was hollering like mad! We came across together as a three horse photo. It took 10 minutes to decide the finish. My horse won! Half boos and half cheers. The riders who pinned me down tried to claim a foul against me. Ten *more* minutes and the three of us sat in dead silence before they made the results official.

Latonia Racetrack, now Turfway Park in Florence, Kentucky, held a big promotion and invited Steve Cauthen, the youngest rider to ever win the Triple Crown, to their track to race. It was his big night—born and raised in Kentucky—he was the favorite. I was the only woman riding and right at the end of the race, my horse just pulled away and I beat him. That wasn't supposed to happen. A woman was *not* supposed to beat Steve Cauthen!

In the summer of 1969, I rode Delaware Park racetrack. Negative crowds were common, but one fan heckled me every single day for two months. "Girl, go home, you need to make babies, you need to cook dinner, clean your house, you have no right to be riding." I never looked at his face. I looked straight ahead. A cute but tough little girl, 4' 10" or so, from the rough side of the tracks came in to help around the stable. She said, "Diane, we gotta get that man." She would always defend me when people said negative things about me. I told her to ignore them, especially that man.

When we went to Atlantic City, she came with us. One morning, I said to her, "This may be the first time we don't have to listen to that jackass who was at Delaware Park hollering at us."

Remembering him, she said, "Yea, I am so sick of that man I could punch him out." And wouldn't you know, as soon as I got a leg up on my horse, there he was—heckling and screaming. That little gal went up to him and punched the living hell out of him, right dead in the face. She knocked him down, gave him a nosebleed and broke his glasses into a million pieces. He got up and didn't even realize who punched him. Not another word from him after that. She said to me, "I took care of that man for you. He'll never yell at you again."

In 1970, I made history as the first woman to ever ride in the Kentucky Derby. I had been in the top ten standings at Churchill Downs but the Derby claimed my fame. The atmosphere at the Kentucky Derby is electric, an experience unto itself. What a week! I was approached by a horse owner from Louisville. He was holding his hat in his hand, as polite as any Southern gentleman could be. "Would you be kind enough to ride my horse in the Derby?" I couldn't believe it. A millionaire who owned whiskey distilleries was asking me to ride his horse in the Kentucky Derby! Oh yes, I wanted to ride in that Derby! I wanted to win that Derby! It was so overpowering—a challenge and a thrill. I didn't win the race, but I didn't come in last either. According to the Derby Museum, I was in contention until the 8th pole.

My brother was on the other side of the world in Vietnam, sitting in the barracks listening to the Armed Forces Network radio. To his astonishment, his sister was racing in the Kentucky Derby.

After many more years of riding, I suffered my big injury, the one that could keep me from riding. I had a lot of injuries over the years, but not like this one. I got pinned under my horse and the bones in my left leg were fractured and my ankle was crushed. My prognosis was never to ride again. Laid up in bed, I was contacted by a wonderful organization, the Don McBeth Foundation. They offered to pay my medical expenses. Phone calls and cards came pouring in from fans everywhere. I couldn't believe the support and love coming my way, so I decided to try to race once more. My doctor warned me not to do it. With braces on my legs, I looked like a bionic woman on my horse! A few years went by and I knew I had to stop. The pain was too much to bear.

I had spent a lifetime devoted to horses and decided to put my knowledge to use in equine sales, helping others pursue their dreams. For me, my dream was fulfilled on every ride...on every horse that was competitive, giving me everything, riding toward a win...knowing the power under you is trying just as hard as you are.

Military

WILMA L. VAUGHT

Brigadier General Wilma L. Vaught, USAF, Retired, served in the United States Air Force for over 28 years, retiring in 1985 as one of the most highly decorated women in U.S. history, having been awarded the Defense and Air Force Distinguished Service Medals, Air Force Legion of Merit, Bronze Star, Meritorious Service Medal, Joint Service Commendation Medal, Air Force Commendation Medal with Oak Leaf Cluster, Republic of Vietnam Gallantry Cross with palm, Republic of Vietnam Campaign Medal and Vietnam Service Award with four stars. She is also the first woman to command a unit receiving the Joint Meritorious Unit Award.

Her distinctive achievements list is long and includes many "firsts" with national organizations such as the Women's International Center, International Women's Forum, National Women's Hall of Fame, Women's History Project, and National Organization for Women (NOW).

She was also the first woman to head a board of directors of a major credit union.

Throughout her career, she forged new paths and pioneered opportunities for the servicewomen who would follow. A Vietnam veteran, she was one of the few military women in that war who were not nurses. She was also the first female Air Force officer to attend the Industrial College of the Armed Forces.

When she was promoted to brigadier general in 1980, she was one of a handful of women in the world to ever achieve that distinction.

The many firsts she achieved helped pave the way for thousands of other military women to be judged based on their abilities, not their gender.

While her military accomplishments are extraordinary, General Vaught's most lasting contribution will be her successful efforts in a campaign that raised some $22.5 million to build the Women In Military Service For America Memorial in Washington, D.C. Because of her, the American people and visitors from around the world can learn of the courage, bravery and accomplishments of tens of thousands of American women who, like General Vaught, have pioneered the future.

The Way I See It...

No matter how tough the job, you don't give up. You must persevere.

Courage

I grew up in a man's world.

I was the older of two girls, born in 1930, who lived on a farm in rural Scotland, Illinois. We knew the value of hard work because we had very little money. I helped my father and went out with the horses and the tractor to help get the ground ready for planting and then later to harvest the crops. I lived a different life during high school compared to a typical teenage girl in the city in 1948, I can assure you.

My parents were truthful people who believed in helping others. A major difference between my parents was that my mother loved to read and my father wasn't interested in reading. I became a reader and I believe that was a major factor in my life. I read the *Bobbsey Twins*, *Nancy Drew* and comics like *Batman* and *Superman*.

I have worked hard to make people understand that you need an education. Reading is critical to education and having a successful career.

When I graduated, my high school had the largest graduating class ever at 24 … 12 boys and 12 girls, most of whom went all 12 years together. We are still friends to this day, at least those still living.

I went on to graduate from the University of Illinois in 1952 and although I immediately found a job in the corporate world, I saw little possibility for managerial advancement. After reading an Army recruiting appeal that offered the opportunity to be a manager and supervisor, I joined the Air Force!

My parents thought I would never make it in the military service because they didn't think I took orders too well.

There were few women in the service in 1957 and the environment was very male oriented. Based on my work on the farm with my father and my experience in my post-college job, I was accustomed to this environment.

In the military was where my career really took off and I would realize my desire to manage and supervise, i.e., be in charge.

At the time, it was probably an advantage to be a woman. At one of the bases where I was stationed, I was one of four women. If I did well, it really stood out, but if I did poorly, it would have shown too. I probably received more recognition because I was different and stood out compared to males.

An obstacle from time to time was the lack of restroom facilities for women, if you can believe it. This is just one small example of the difficulties of being a woman in a man's military.

During my career, I held many positions in the comptroller field at bases in the United States, Spain, and Vietnam. Toward the end, I served as chairperson of the NATO Women in the Allied Forces Committee and was the senior woman military representative to the Defense Advisory Committee on Women in the Services. My last assignment was as Commander of the U.S. Military Entrance Processing Command in Chicago, the largest geographical command in the military.

My military experience gave me an opportunity to participate in historic events, broaden my education and work with a committed group of people who are fascinating, dedicated, well-educated and who almost never say "can't" and never say "won't"! When I look back, there are people I would now classify as mentors for every stage of my career. They guided me whether I wanted to be or not, and they consisted of both men and women.

One in particular stands out the most: Lt. Ruth Blind at Barksdale Air Force Base, La., my first base. She had served in World War II and was a personnel expert. She educated me and taught me how to recognize the things you needed to do in the military. She took me under her wing and had me doing things others frequently never had an opportunity to do. I did investigative work for administrative boards—something I was less than enthusiastic about doing. She told me it was something I needed to do. She was a tremendous person and my first mentor and role model in the military.

When I became a *lieutenant,* I recognized that I was a role model, too. I was very aware that people were constantly watching me. I therefore have always tried to do the right thing, no matter how painful it is to me. Doing the right thing when faced with a hard decision might not be the easiest way, but to me, it was the only way.

In my life, there is one area I feel I totally failed—my family. My life was the military and I wasn't there many times for my family, but they recognized this and understood that my job was of paramount importance to me and all other things were secondary.

An important door opened for me and other women in the military in 1967 when President Lyndon Johnson signed into law a measure finally permitting women to be promoted to the level of general and admiral. That same law also lifted the quotas that had been placed on women being promoted to the General and Flag officer ranks, which also allowed for new career opportunities.

In 1980, my father had the honor of pinning a star on my shoulder when I became the first woman in the comptroller field to be promoted to brigadier general. Two years later, I was made the commander of one of the largest geographical commands in the military. When I retired in 1985, I was one of only three female generals in the Air Force and one of seven in the U.S. Armed Forces.

I serve now as a member of the Board of Directors of the National Women's History Museum and on the Virginia War Memorial Foundation Board of Trustees. In addition, I have worked as a consultant with the Strategic Defense Initiative Organization as well as industry. I speak around the country on leadership and management and I am frequently on radio and television programs.

As president of the Women's Memorial Foundation, I believe we have a message to tell and that is the story of women's service. This is what I have worked for since my retirement … not to tell my story, but the stories of what others have done, their history, their progress. On October 18, 1997, the Women In Military Service For America Memorial, standing at the gateway to Arlington National Cemetery, was dedicated. Some 40,000 women veterans and their families and friends gathered to honor the past, present and future of women in the military. It is the nation's only major memorial to pay tribute to the more than 2.5 million women who have served in our nation's defense, beginning with the American Revolution. It stands as a place where America's servicewomen can take their rightful place in history and where their stories will be told for future generations.

The Memorial is important for servicewomen because if you don't understand where you've been, you may not understand where you're going. We need to know what women have done and are capable of doing. It is not too much to believe that one day, we will have a woman president/commander-in-chief, shattering this significant piece of the glass ceiling.

I firmly believe women are far more capable than some expect or give credit.

My favorite poem, *Courage*, by Amelia Earhart, is one I memorized in high school and it is meaningful to me because I have faced many difficult decisions and have thought back to that poem to get me through. Every time we make a choice, we are influencing what the rest of our lives are going to be…for the rest of the day…for the rest of the hour…or for our future.

Courage is the price that
Life exacts for granting peace.
The soul that knows it not
Knows no release from little things:

Knows not the livid loneliness of fear,
Nor mountain heights where bitter joy can hear the sound of wings.

How can life grant us boon of living, compensate
For dull gray ugliness and pregnant hate
Unless we dare
The soul's dominion.

Each time we make a choice, we pay
With courage to behold resistless day,
And count it fair.

The first and last verses say so much about living.

Comedy

"Cherish forever what makes you unique,
'cuz you're really a yawn if it goes!"

—Bette Midler
American entertainer

PHYLLIS DILLER

Phyllis Diller is the longest-running comedienne in history. Her name is synonymous with comedy. She began her career in 1955 at the Purple Onion in San Francisco. In 1967, the renowned comedian, Bob Hope, liked "her old face" and put her in his movie, Eight on the Lam. *It was the start of a lifelong friendship between the two, resulting in decades of laughter for audiences worldwide.*

Never slowing down, her late-in-life artistic endeavor has produced one dynamic 90-something year old.

Phyllis lives in her sprawling estate in Brentwood, California, continually giving back to her community and beyond.

The Way I See It...

On this happy day, I am thankful for my blessings and I pray for renewed belief in myself and others and hope this bond of love will expand to envelop the entire universe.

Still Joking Around

When I think of my greatest achievement in life, I have to say it was being the breadwinner of a homeless family. Nobody asked me to do it or forced me to do it. Somebody had to work. Somebody had to figure it out. I was the only one able. Everyone was looking at me. You can't let little babies take over and my husband couldn't take over…he couldn't even leave the house.

He was not dumb. My husband was mentally ill and I didn't realize it until I was about 80 years old and he had been dead for years. I just didn't know what was wrong with the man. He was very sick. I knew there was something wrong with him but I didn't realize that he had no control.

I had five children and a husband to take care of. That's what launched my career.

It was a good thing that I was like my father. He was a fine salesman. He could sell ice cubes to Siberians! He had a wonderful personality and knew how to present himself to people. When I started working in Oakland, California, I was doing the same thing my father did, but at a radio station. It was promotion work…which is simply an extension of sales. I started out just like a lot of other girls at the radio station.

And then, of course, came Bob Hope. He was absolutely the biggest influence in my career. And he loved me! I had worshipped him as a teenager on radio. I was a huge fan. I never realized he would be someone I would be friends with. We had great chemistry too. He thought I was great…I thought he was God.

He helped my career so much. Putting me in three of his movies didn't hurt at all! And I appeared most often as the *woman* in his television specials. That was big. If I wasn't in the show, his writers would always write about me. In every monologue, there was something about Phyllis Diller. He just loved me.

For women just starting out today and entering college, I would have to advise them to work their tail off and study like a mad person. Do your very best and get straight "A's." When you get out, get a job you can learn from. You can learn something on *every* job…learn from the ground up because that may be the job where you end up as the CEO.

Women today are looking for their purpose. Once they find that position, they can find their own way. Plan it one step at a time. A trip around the world begins with the first step.

Never give up either. Sometimes a person has to go through some kinds of hell to a better place. Hillary Clinton is an example of true grit… she wants to be the first woman president. I don't think she's going to do it, but we're going to care a lot that she is making all the right moves. It is impressive to see what she's done…my, my, to live through her marriage took a lot of class…to just let it settle and go on in life…how cheap her husband was…how awful…talk about no class!

My greatest challenge now is my old age. I'm faking it you know. I have doctors' appointments and everything starts to turn into a crumbling ruin. It's a drag to not be youthful, but I can't complain. Complaining makes it worse.

That old English poem's first line, "My mind is my kingdom," is one of my all time favorites. I loved that line 80 years ago and it's still true. It's still vibrating. I will continue to get so many fabulous ideas…new ideas…I will think about them…I will write jokes about funny situations. My mind really is my kingdom.

Just last night, I painted until midnight. I have my own art gallery and I just sold a painting for a thousand dollars! And I have another one up for sale at $200,000. So you see, I have things to do.

On this happy day, I am thankful for my blessings and I pray for renewed belief in myself and others and hope this bond of love will expand to envelop the entire universe.

I see a lot of people my age and they all have rheumatism. I have it too, but it doesn't hurt and I think that has something to do with my mind. I just don't *habit hurting*.

I know I am blessed. I just can't believe it.

Most people would be surprised to know I am an atheist, but it is really just a matter of nomenclature. I am a very spiritual person. I believe in spirits but I don't believe in organized religions. I could say more about this, but my mother taught me to "keep your own counsel," which means don't spill everything and don't think you have to be talking all the time.

Listen more. I wish I hadn't been such a blabbermouth, I guess. I learned this late in life. Silence really is golden and people who talk all the time aren't learning anything. When you get with a group of people, you can hear each one trying to top each other. It's silly…it's dumb…and I learned finally not to do it.

At this stage of my life, I stay busy. It is just incredible. I constantly receive flowers, go out like four nights a week to some top dinner spot and I'm having a blast, a wonderful life! I see people like the former mayor and his wife and the former governor Pete Wilson and his wife...they're all interesting people and just adorable...and they take me out!

I don't have to worry about reinventing myself. I'm just out there and they still want me to tell them jokes.

"You can't be brave if you've only had wonderful things happen to you."

—*Mary Tyler Moore*
American actress

ESTHER PAIK GOODHART

Not too many people can claim to be both Korean and Jewish.

Born in the heart of Texas, Esther Paik Goodhart is the daughter of a famous 100% Korean Presbyterian minister, Doctor the Most Divine Reverend John Yewon Paik, and his wife, the Korean Tammy Faye Bakker. Who knew Esther would grow up to be a hilarious Jewish comic?

A tortuous childhood sent her straight to comedy, performing and winning awards and contests from New York to California. She also has enjoyed success as a playwright with her one-woman Off-Broadway play, Out of the Wheelchair and Into the Fire. *The self-described "Oriental Beauty Jewess" is a regular personality on* WOR *radio and can be seen frequently on television in commercials, documentaries, made-for-TV movies, and as host of a* PBS *television talk show. She's even a cartoon on the* Food Network.

Esther's greatest thrill is her membership to the famed Friars Club, where she enjoys being with people "who don't call her Mommy."

Milton Berle once told her, "Don't let the bastards get you down." She took that advice and ran with it.

The Way I See It...

You have to listen to the God, the spirit, that's in your heart. It's there. Listen.

From Out of the Wheelchair

My father taught me to play the piano by the "hit or miss" method. If I missed a note, he would hit me...usually with a bat, maybe a frying pan. He would take me out to the car and break my finger if I didn't play the piano correctly. And then tell me not to cry.

People are usually surprised to hear me speak this way about my father. "How can you talk badly about one of the greatest leaders of the community?"

It is true—he was a great leader, but a horrible father. Fame and fortune usually come with a tremendous cost and the children pay a high price. Many celebrities give so much of themselves to the public, they have nothing left for their family.

My father would always say to me, "You are a mistake. God punished me with you!"

Now, I say, "I know I am going to heaven because I spent my time in hell."

My parents considered me a curse, a punishment and a burden because I was born with a neurological disorder called Familial Dystonia. They were Korean War immigrants, with a different way of viewing humanity than the western way, especially the American way. In North Korea in the 1950s, if you had disabled children, you discarded them. You put them in the field and let nature take over. If you were *poor,* your handicapped children were really looked down upon. They drained the community. To have a child that was disabled and slowly dying was emotionally draining too. In America, women and children had rights, but in the Asian community, it was different. Rights were difficult to preserve in a developing country. You couldn't afford to keep a disabled child. My parents didn't see me as just a drain. They went beyond that. I was their personal infliction, their blight. My father would say that I was "worse than dog. At least you can *eat* dog!"

As I see it, I represent every oppressed group in need of affirmative action in America. I am a woman, disabled, a minority and a veteran, if you consider the time I spent in my parents' house as my personal Vietnam.

My parents had four girls and two of us were handicapped. We would fall behind while my father carried my two non-handicapped sisters and walked ahead of us…a whole block ahead. He said, "If you don't catch up with me, never come home." Naturally, we thought we were going to be abandoned, afraid we would never make it home. From this horrendous experience I have an unerring sense of direction.

My father didn't want me to have a wheelchair, so he forced me to walk and try to look normal. He would say, "Shake it off and don't embarrass me with you sitting in a wheelchair." But of course, I needed one and my first dream was to get out of it! If I could get out of the wheelchair, I believed everything would be great. I was given my wheelchair in high school, where, of course, a wheelchair becomes a *contraceptive* because no boy would touch me while I sat in one.

My greatest act of courage has been getting out of the chair and hiding my dependence on it. They say when you are out of the wheelchair, the wheelchair is still in your head. But when my son was born, he pushed that chair right out of my head. My son was God's blessing.

God has always given me strength. He gave me strength to see that I was *not* a curse or a punishment to my parents. I also understood, with God's help, that we are all His children and perfect in His eyes—if not in the eyes of my own father. When my father said that my handicap made me imperfect I said, "God is perfect. God made me. So, I *am* perfect."

At times, I would be in the hospital for months near death from my Dystonia. When I returned home after one hospital stay, my father became so frustrated, he beat me. He took my boot and beat me on the head until I bled from my inner ear. I went back to the hospital with my mother. When they asked what happened, she said I fell. Hospital workers were suspicious. They found it odd that I would come in with so many problems.

My father made it a habit to beat me with the buckle side of the belt because it would hurt more. Cuts, bruises and whelps on my body were common. I learned to say that my injuries came from falling down. Because of my handicap, everyone believed my excuse.

I knew how I hurt myself falling down—if only everyone else could have. My father would throw me down the steps, from the second floor to the first. He even threw me from the first floor to the basement where the steps had metal edges. He had a pretty warped sense of *good* parenting. His way of discipline was to instill fear in me.

Child protection services didn't exist at that time. But, when TV's *Phil Donahue Show* urged abuse victims to speak out, I called my Caucasian minister. "My father is beating me and I need help."

The minister called my father and my father screamed at me. "How dare you speak to anyone about my business!" And he whipped me for telling on him.

The first person to help me was my doctor, Dr. Martin Geller, a neurologist in Queens, New York. When I turned 14, he diagnosed my disorder. Finally, we knew what it was. He assured me it was ridiculous to think this was "God's punishment." He knew when I came to see him all beaten and bloody that it was not normal. He pulled me out of the closet in terms of speaking out for my health rights and learning about my illness. I became an educated patient, and I still see Dr. Geller to this day.

Other parents treated their handicapped children so differently. On the yellow school bus, there were far more physically disabled children than my sister and me. Parents would run from their houses to meet the bus. Kissing and hugging their children, they would tell them, "I love you!" I couldn't believe it. I never heard my parents say they loved me. When I got off the bus, my mom would rush me into the house and try to hide me. She was ashamed.

I never understood why I was alive. Too many times my disabled classmates would die. Their families would be devastated. I would cry out to God, "Why didn't you take me? These parents want their child. My parents don't want me! Let *me* die so I can make everyone happy."

God doesn't want me with Him yet. I think He is afraid that I will make too much noise in heaven. Heaven can wait because I have work to do on earth. Whatever my pain, others have had worse.

When I was 21, the doctors wanted to give me a hysterectomy because they believed, due to my handicap, I should never have children. I agreed. I couldn't take care of myself, how would I be able to take care of a child? But something always came up and I never had the operation. After five miscarriages, I had my first son at age 33! I thought my miscarriages were God's way of telling me that I should adopt a puppy! Now we have two sons—two gorgeous, smart, healthy, low-maintenance boys.

My husband Alan is my earth angel. He married me despite the fact I was in a wheelchair. He thought *he* was lucky to be married to me! What a romantic…he bought me different colored wheelchairs to match whatever outfit I wore. In the throes of my disability, lying on the floor crying from the pain, he would tell me I was brave.

When people ask me what is the secret to our 28 years of marriage I tell them that it is because Alan is willing to be wrong all the time. Alan married his "Miss Right," but he didn't know my first name is "Always." After one of my drama queen episodes would die down and I came back to my senses, I realized what an idiot I was…and I'm grateful that my husband allows me to figure that out for myself.

When my father found out Alan wanted to marry me, he thought I was insane. First of all, a Jew? I'm the first born in America. I come from a line of phenomenal people who were aristocrats in Korea and prospered in the United States. My father was a famous minister; my uncle a very famous physics professor in America; and another uncle was a famous artist. How dare I go against tradition and not marry a Korean man? Alan was even unemployed, looking for work in construction. I said to my father, "Your boss was an unemployed Jewish carpenter born on Christmas day. Alan is an unemployed Jewish carpenter and his birthday happens to be on Christmas day!" My father decided he was going to be the father-in-law of the Messiah and we raced each other down the aisle to get to Alan first!

When my father died, because I am the first-born, it was my duty to plan everything. I bought the coffin, gave the eulogy and housed and fed 2,000 people three days in a row. He died on Saturday but we had to keep him refrigerated until Thursday so that all the dignitaries around the world could come.

It was an open coffin service. Many in the Korean community came to the funeral and they felt compelled to touch my father, kiss my father, climb into the casket with my father…they cried and mourned my father's passing, but I had no tears for him. He was my tormentor. I couldn't remember anything good that he ever did for me.

Then I remembered that the last thing my father said to me before he died was that I was fat. That's when I cried. I have always been sensitive about my weight. I am an oppressed minority: a Korean woman who weighs over 90 pounds. Until that moment I was dry-eyed at his funeral. Without warning, I was weeping uncontrollably. Suddenly, I was surrounded by Korean women who wanted to know what was wrong.

I sobbed, "My father said I was fat!" The women pleaded with me not to weep and assured me, "Oh, no, Esther you not fat. Stop cry. You not fat." After many assurances, I calmed down and stopped crying.

Then I heard, "But Esther, *why* you so fat?"

That struck me as so funny. I began to laugh. I laughed so hard, my mind opened. My father *did* do something wonderful for me! He gave me a powerful name that I try daily to live up to, and he gave me my total lack of fear of death. He taught me many good things. I never say, "Why me?" when bad things happen to me, because I never say "Why me?" when wonderful things happen to me. From a cruel parent, I learned how to be a good parent. From a parent with no patience, I learned patience. I should thank my teacher—my father taught me what *not* to do. He also made me read the Bible, where I found many examples of bad parenting. Take Abraham, for example. Here's a father who was willing to kill his son because God ordered it. Saul tried to kill his son, Jonathan, at the dinner table for sticking up for his friend David. Even our Lord God sent his own son to hang on the cross and suffer. I learned that good can come from suffering. I learned that from the sacrifices of Jonathan, Isaac and Jesus, the world became a better place. I learned that we all have the ability to rise above our own personal hardship and suffering to make things better for ourselves and others. If I am Christ-like in that sense, then we *all* are. We all have the ability to bring out the God in ourselves and others.

My father had a special ability. Knowing this helps me forgive him. As a famous religious leader, he accomplished many marvelous things for the community. He may have sacrificed his own family and children, like parents in the Bible, but he was nevertheless a great religious leader who taught me to lead. Through his example, my father inspired me to dedicate my life to serving communities nationwide. Service is the rent I pay to live in this great country.

I went from sitting in a wheelchair to doing stand-up comedy...in high heels! It's a miracle. I used to see my wheelchair as a prison, but then I understood that I needed it. It helped me. Without it, I would not have been able to get around. It also helped me get married. As I said earlier, I met my husband when I was still in the wheelchair, seriously handicapped. Nevertheless, I had something no other woman who had dated my husband had—handicapped parking!

My life is the *Book of Esther*. Such horror and suffering, but look at the delight. Am I blessed or what?

Communications

NANCY GILES

Since 2003, Nancy Giles has been a contributor to CBS News' Sunday Morning *television show. She describes it as a "beautiful show with a slow pace." That certainly does not describe this woman's life and career as one of the "first women of color" to encounter the glass ceiling, which she aptly describes as being a "cement ceiling."*

As an actress, she was in the ensemble cast of ABC-TV's Emmy-Award winning series, China Beach, *and in the film* Working Girl. *She was the announcer and sometime co-host of* Fox After Breakfast *and has enjoyed success on the radio with* The Jay Thomas Morning Show *based in New York City and the Gracie-award winning* Giles and Moriarty *in Philadelphia.*

The Way I See It...

I think it's important to know that you can't have it all, but you can have more at different times.

A Unique and Sassy Girl

I'm the fifth of seven kids. We grew up in Queens, New York, in a house with a big yard. Our house didn't have plastic covers on the furniture, so all the kids loved coming over and hanging out and having a fun time. There was always stuff going on at our house.

My mom was an artist, a dress maker, an art teacher and a music lover...a very creative person. My father is an architect who also loves music. Either the radio was on or records were playing. Reading was important too. We had lots of books, and we would get into arguments about different volumes of the encyclopedia like, "Who's hogging volume S?" We had a lot of fun with reading.

I found a note I had written in the fourth grade. Apparently, I wanted to be a best selling author. I loved writing. I looked at the note and thought, wow, I *did* have thoughts like that. It surprised me because I just remember enjoying being a kid and not thinking that far ahead.

In the first grade, I calculated how old I would be when I graduated from college. I love that...it was already on my mind! I thought about what I was going to do, but not as much as *who I was going to be with*! I didn't have any fantasies about my husband or boyfriend. I just wondered who it might be. I had tiny dreams about acting because I was kind of shy and quiet. My memory is vague, but I remember how much fun it was making people laugh. I can't say that I was driven to do anything, except maybe writing. I am not one of those people that could say I knew I wanted to be an actor at age five. The writing, though. That was there early on.

My family members were my mentors. My older brother Lee went away to college and I wrote him a letter about the first day of school in fifth grade. He wrote back and said, among other things, "I loved your letter. It captured the exact feelings I remember." That made me really happy. I looked up to my older sister, Lorna, who went to MIT, and my other brother who went to Boston University. They got college scholarships and they achieved and worked hard. My father was the first in his family to graduate from college. My mom was awarded an art scholarship but didn't graduate. She left to enlist in the women's army corp in the forties.

My mom was true grit. She passed away about ten years ago. She was very proud of me. My father is too. I believe my brothers and sisters are proud of me. Other people show it in different ways.

Quite a bit of sacrifice goes with success. I didn't intend to be 48 years old and single, with no kids and not even a steady. I thought I would be married and have kids by now. It would be nice to have a boyfriend at some point. Hopefully, my sister has forgiven me because I missed her wedding. I was doing a show in New York, an important show. They didn't have an understudy for me. I still feel badly, but I think as time goes by, you start figuring out what you can, and can't do. At that time, I would never say no to anything. Now, I look at a calendar and try to carve out time. For example, I am going to that same sister's daughter's high school graduation soon. Circumstances led me back to New York about a year and a half before my mom was diagnosed with ovarian cancer, and I had a flexible enough schedule that I was able to go with her to chemo treatments and just be around her.

Getting older changes your perspective. It's beautiful...it's wonderful.

In many ways women have reached the glass ceiling. And I do believe there is a glass ceiling. Glass is a nice metaphor, because it seems like you can see through it to the other side. There have been times when I felt like it was a cement ceiling. It's been really rough for me.

I was at Second City in Chicago, an absolute breakthrough for me... improvisational comedy taught me so much about writing and life.... how to handle different things that are coming your way. However, comedy can be kind of sexist. In our group, there were four or five men and only two women. I fought very hard to get a company with three women but was met with all kinds of resistance. I was also one of the women of color there. This was 25 years ago. It was very hard then and it's still hard today. It's a very male dominated field and there are some men, even some famous men, who think they are better than women. I believe the noted author Christopher Hitchens wrote a piece that talked about how women aren't funny. And yeah, they are! You have to have an amazing sense of humor just to *be* a woman. In the south, north, east, west, urban or rural, you couldn't make it through life without a sense of humor. And the ones that don't, have a tougher time.

I didn't succeed at Second City the way I wanted. They had a big-shot touring company that I wanted to make the main stage with, and I auditioned a few times, but acting and performing is very subjective. They felt I wasn't ready. I felt I was, and so, I quit. I felt slighted. Being a woman and a *black* woman had something to do with it. At that time, they had not had a black woman in their main stage company, period. I was very unhappy not being able to get where I wanted. In not getting there, I learned a tremendous lesson. It brought me back to New York and then I was determined!

Some opportunities have changed for minorities, yet some have stayed the same. Just because things have changed a little bit, people assume that everything's fine.

Nothing is truly wrong with the entertainment business…and every industry has an extra consciousness about making sure women and people of color are represented. I don't see that as tokenism. It isn't anything other than reflecting the true America. Oprah Winfrey's best friend Gayle King said, "You need to remember who you are." I agree.

You also can't give up. I love the word *grit*. It's one of those onomonapoetic words that sound like what it is. You have to *grit* your teeth to say the word, a bite-down, take no prisoners, by any means necessary approach. You know what I mean. Get it done! Don't forget humor, though. Humor must go along with grit.

Interesting dynamics happen on *Sunday Morning* when I have to double assert myself. It's important since I'm a woman *and* a woman of color. Not too many people look like me in my position and are free to express an opinion. This is a gift to me from CBS. At certain times, I know my take is going to be different, so I launch it! My heart is pounding and my head is hurting and I worry about ruffling feathers or people not liking me, but I'm getting old enough now to just go with it.

I think it is wonderful having Hillary Clinton and even more so, Barack Obama, in such prominent positions in this year's presidential election. All of a sudden, on television, almost every network is finding people of color to get their take on things. And not just one…it's more than one. It's fantastic!

I don't want any young women to be offended by what I am about to say, but if there are things that you want to achieve, it's imperative that you get an education. It's also imperative to use birth control because the statistics for teenage pregnancies is alarming. Don't get me wrong, I'm not against children. I love children. I was going to have a child and I think people can have children and have a career and husband. But there has to be a balance. You can't really have it all. You have to weigh certain options. Just be careful with relationships when you are young. Understand the issue of pregnancy, because that will knock you out of being able to continue with your education and focus on your career. Know that you can't have it all but you can have more at different times. Keep the idea of balance. Women have to do much more than men. Men have a way of carrying on their careers and coming home where everything is done. For women, it's tough.

Don't worry if every woman you meet along the way doesn't help you. I hate to say that, but I used to feel that every black woman must feel the same as I do about issue x or y, but they don't. Some of the people who helped me and were kind to me in my career were white men. Some of the best scripts I have read from a "woman's point of view" were written by men! It's finding like-minded people and being able to work with them that is the most important thing.

Never forget your family and friends. I score touchdowns with my family. They are the ones I call in the middle of the night.

I loved acting, but I love doing this kind of commentary and opinion on *Sunday Morning*. It's such a charge for me when I meet people and they say, "I really like how you think."

One day, I am going to get myself organized enough to write a book. That way, when it's all over and I'm gone, maybe I can be remembered as an interesting, unique-minded, opinionated, sassy girl with opinions!

Advertising

"People think at the end of the day that a man is the only answer [to fulfillment].
Actually a job is better for me."

—*Diana Frances Spencer*
(1961–1997) Princess of Wales & Duchess of Rothesay

ANNE TOLSTOI WALLACH

*Anne Wallach started her 30 year advertising career in 1949,
eventually becoming the first woman Creative Director at J. Walter
Thompson in New York City. It was the largest advertising company
in the world at the time. Her work won many awards, including the
Grand Prix at the Cannes Film Festival. In an industry-wide magazine
contest, she won first prize—an Arizona ghost town renamed for
her. She managed the first advertising campaign for NOW (National
Organization of Women), which was added to Radcliffe's Schlesinger
Library of Women's Studies. She also served as the first woman executive
board member of the American Arbitration Association.*

At age 50, she wrote Women's Work, *a novel which dealt with
barriers to top positions for women. That book earned her the highest
advance ever paid to an unknown novelist. It became editorial news in*
Newsweek, Fortune *and* People *and was published in 17 languages. She
has written other novels, including* Private Scores. *Her opinion pieces
and book reviews have appeared frequently in the* New York Times.

*In 2004, she became Radcliffe Editor of a Harvard alumni
publication and the first Radcliffe woman to address a Harvard
reunion audience.*

Anne knows a thing or two about cracking a glass ceiling. She was the first to do it in the advertising industry.

The Way I See It...

The shape of women's lives in the second half of the twentieth century is the story of our times. We're coming through it and it's going to be alright.

Breaking the Glass Ceiling

We had the same expectations of ourselves that men had...we were our own prisoners. Everyone thought we would fall in love with the nice boy in the mailroom, quit our jobs, get married and stay home and bring up the children. And we'd be better for it because we'd understand his *work*. The idea that we would do anything ourselves wasn't there. Your parents didn't want you to work if you were a nice girl. If you worked and you were married, everybody thought your husband couldn't support you. You did what your mother and father and husband said to do. What other way was there? Oh, what a mess we were!

When I started my career at J. Walter Thompson, I didn't even think about money. I thought I was lucky because I was working at the biggest agency in the world. I was in the first generation of women in advertising, making $40 to the man's $80. Never did I think to make a comparison. I went to Radcliffe, considered even then a part of Harvard. I had the same education as the men at Thompson and never thought twice about it. Our ideas kept us down, not just the situations.

Thompson was rigid...no girl ever started higher than a secretary. You could get to copyrighter or art director but that was it. Never an exccutive. The women's group was segregated, on a separate floor. Theoretically, you would get further with your own kind, rather than having men step on you, or "making love to you." They were terrified of that and told you on your very first day if you ever got involved with a man, you would get fired and he would remain. To be warned! We wore hats to distinguish ourselves from the secretaries and maids brought lunches on trays to us.

A floor was dedicated as a resting or napping area, a sort of medical center. Men could be a little sick, maybe with a hangover. A large space was dedicated for women and staffed with a lady nurse. As a woman, you were expected to have the vapors at strange times, having your period or whatever. With her alarm clock nearby, the nurse would tuck you into a blanket, give you a pillow and soothe you for an hour or two. She would wake you when you wanted. It was such an insane thing if you consider the cost of office space.

The company's dining room had been brought over piece by piece from London, fabulous décor. On Wednesdays, the men "left it to the women." We couldn't go any other time and we didn't argue about it. We thought it was nice they let us come once a week.

The stories can be funny, although they're very serious, because we're talking about something that is unfair to half the population. But it is lost history because people don't know it and they don't always believe it. They ask me why did you put up with it? Why didn't you complain? There was no machinery for complaining and you got into a multitude of trouble if you did. The prevailing attitude was "women were lucky to have a job in this wonderful place. Don't make waves. Nice women don't make waves."

People would ask me, "Why can't you be more like *Ruth*?" There were so many *Ruths* at Thompson. Everyone thought *Ruth* was so sweet. She did whatever you asked her to do. *Ruth* was a jerk!

I worked within the rules because I couldn't work without them. I encouraged change, too. My office was fantastic, an elegant place filled with art, a real Chippendale table, Queen Anne chairs, formality and manners, and I swear, a crystal chandelier. We were treated very special, as in, "You don't want to bother your pretty head about that." And you did! That's why you were there.

President Nixon's future Chief of Staff Bob Haldeman used to tell me what women want. He was the account executive on the hair removal product, Nair. He was convinced he knew what women would buy and he was dead wrong. I would try to tell him but he was the boss.

When I worked on the Scott Paper account and my ads starting winning awards, my boss took the account away from me and gave it to a bunch of men. Of course, I had to train those same men. An elderly man on the account, maybe 65 years old, had gone for the first time to a supermarket. He was fascinated. "It's wonderful!" he said. "They put these little babies in carts and their little legs stick out, and the mothers put the food in the basket and they don't have to leave their children." I said to myself, I do this every day of my life. We were a different species. We would laugh, what else could you do?

And we'd cry. We cried a lot.

Early on, I worked on a product called Trushay, a hand lotion. The ads featured beautiful pictures of a woman's hands with the bottle pouring drops from above and she is rubbing the *backs* of her hands together. These were Irving Penn pictures that cost a fortune. I finally told my boss, "That isn't the way women put on hand lotion…you put it in your *palms* and then rub." He said, "That doesn't look very pretty." Women started writing letters to us saying, "That is not the way you put on hand lotion." It took collaboration for anybody to believe me. I had to be proved right over and over and over. I found myself constantly saying, "Women don't do that, women do this."

The executives who made a great deal of money had very little idea of what went on in life. They lived in places on the railroad line…Greenwich, beautiful places in New Jersey. They came in to Grand Central where the office was, came upstairs and then went home. They played golf on the weekends and never read the newspapers. You would have to take the *New York Times* into meetings and show them things…they weren't worldly at all. The president of J. Walter said to me, "I know you wrote this campaign and you think it's very good, but if you were a woman, would you really want to do it this way?" I thought, he's talking to me but not *seeing* me. He was saying, you're not a housewife woman. You're a sophisticated New York woman, not really one of *them*. I was an alien species.

Only men attended meetings until I came along. They said "Good morning" to each other, but to me they would say, "Why, Anne, don't you look pretty this morning?" They were terrified of women, afraid of what we were going to do. If you cried, they didn't know what to do. It was a very poor idea to cry because it scared them and they never wanted to be around you again.

I worked all the way through three pregnancies. I had my second child as I left the office on a Friday afternoon. I worked until a week before my third one was born and went back three weeks later. You had your babies on vacation. When I was working for ad executive David Ogilvy, he wouldn't let me come to a meeting because I was pregnant. He felt it was unlucky and unseemly to be in the room. I could do the work in the back room but I wasn't to come out. I suppose you would have been absolutely burned at the stake if you breastfed. They judged everything by their wives and had no idea of what reality was like.

There were other women on the bandwagon but I didn't get much help from my sisters anywhere along the way. There was an attitude of, "I got here. Now you go and do your thing." I also heard younger girls say about me, "She's old and she doesn't know what she's doing and I can sweet talk this guy and get him to do what I want." People can be rotten.

When I wrote my book, *Women's Work*, Charlotte Curtis on the *New York Times* staff wrote a review of it and absolutely savaged it. She hated the book and hated that my heroine cried. She was a top columnist at the time and the kind of woman who had always followed the rules exactly. She never helped anybody. She couldn't bear it that I had written a different point of view from her own. That was the general attitude of women. I got much more help from men than I ever got from women. There were a few good men who treated me like a person and not like an exotic flower or a nut.

The Revsons of Revlon Cosmetics were tough to work with, but at least they didn't sugar coat things. They would throw an ad on the floor and say, "Who's bringing me this shit?" You would shiver but at least they treated you like a person. They seemed to truly understand women and that was nice.

I got on the Ford automotive account purely by a fluke. The accounts were divided by sex and men had the cars. But there was political pressure to put a woman on the Ford account, so they gave me the least important thing: the Thunderbird in its third year. Cars are made in three year cycles and this was a safe thing to give me. I only had to maintain the advertising. Of course, I started looking for something different and suggested we do a *his and hers* Thunderbird in the Neiman Marcus Christmas catalog. I wanted to put matched luggage and electric curlers in the woman's car and a television and razor in the man's car. Management thought it was a little nuts but it didn't cost much so they let me do it. I worked with Stanley Marcus's brother Edward. He got excited about it. It was a great success. I ended up explaining it to Lee Iacocca in a great big meeting. He addressed us all with, "Good morning *lady* and gentlemen." Now, I stood out in the room. Then he said, "Electric curlers? Isn't that a little low class?" I said, "Oh, no, these are the latest thing, they're Clairol." He said okay and after that, everybody finally started paying attention to me. They let me have the *new* edition of Ford the next year! Even then, the guys never told me where the meetings were. I was always scrambling to get there. One desolate day, I was asked why I never drove the new model around the test track. So I did it. But they were all waiting on me to crash or turn the car over. Little did they know, I didn't even know how to drive!

Nothing was ever even. The worst thing that happened to me was my battle for vice president. There were 16 copy groups at Thompson and I was running one of them. The rest were men. I had as much responsibility; billing, travel, and big clients, but I couldn't get the title. Somebody said, "Just tell her she's a VP…she'll never know the difference. We don't have to make her one." It took me an amazingly long time to get the title and I knew they would never do anything for me again. They figured they'd given me the moon. It was very insulting. I heard it all: women cry, women are emotional and don't come through in a clinch. I kept demonstrating that these things weren't true but nobody ever saw it. Sure, I yelled and cried sometimes, but I endeavored not to.

Feminism was born in the seventies and Thompson offered to do free advertising for the National Organization of Women, NOW, and since I was the only girl in town, I landed the job. Usually, when they did free ads, it was for the Marines. I gathered volunteers, which included the first black woman copywriter at our company. She was smart, stunning and fearless and wore long colorful robes and tall turbans and her name was Shirley Kalunda. We gathered around my table to welcome the executive committee of NOW, five ladies with big hats, big handbags and stern expressions. The president of NOW took over and said our ads must emphasize how shamefully women are treated in the workplace and should tell men they'd better do the right thing. She got wound up and said, "I know ads are supposed to have slogans and I have written one: 'Give women a break. They deserve it and business deserves it, too.'" Dead silence on my side. I saw Shirley rise up to her full height, about 6 feet with turban and say, "F*#^ that. I'm not asking anybody for anything." Nobody talked like that at Thompson. It would take years—and the Sopranos—for women to talk like that.

Two of the most vicious people I have ever met were in that group of women and they did their very best to undermine me like mad, but we finally got all of them to work together and produce some ads that somehow caused a lot of talk and wound up in the Schlesinger Library's collection of women's history. Maybe that helped push things, so that today, women are actually paid 80 percent of what men make for the same work. I even used my Radcliffe diploma in one of the ads that said, "Congratulations, Dad. You've just spent $12,000 so she could join the typing pool."

Legal

JANIE L. SHORES

Justice Janie Shores was elected to the State of Alabama's highest court in 1974, becoming the first female justice on the Alabama Supreme Court. She served almost 25 years on the bench. She also carries the distinction of being the first woman to be elected to an appellate court in America.

After law school, she clerked for Alabama Supreme Court Justice Robert T. Simpson. In 1962, she worked in the legal department of Liberty National Life Insurance Company, and in 1968 became a Professor of Law at Cumberland School of Law.

The Way I See It...

Looking back on my career, I've got to be pleased because there are women on every appellate court in the country now. I never thought of myself as paving the way for women. But I did think: Lord, I'd better not mess up...I would just hate to do something that would discourage women from trying this again in later years.

A Love of Law

For the longest time, I believed that my opinions were discounted because I was not considered old enough to have opinions that counted for much. I longed for the day when I was old enough for people to pay attention to what I had to say. I finally came to realize, though, that it wasn't so much that I was too young...it was that girls' opinions didn't count.

I was raised on a farm in rural Alabama in the 1930s. By the time I started first grade, I already knew nobody cared what I thought about anything...and if that was ever to change...I had to get an education. By third grade, I knew I was smart and had to get one.

There was no money, of course. We picked cotton, strawberries and potatoes. Potatoes were hard, but not as hard as cotton. I worked every summer, moving up from the potato fields to the potato shed.

I graduated high school in 1950, proficient in typing and shorthand. Armed with these new skills, I rode the Greyhound bus to Mobile to look for a job. I was almost 18 years old. I interviewed with the first lawyer I had ever met, Vincent F. Kilborn, Jr. He hired me at a salary of $300 per month...a fortune.

Mr. Kilborn dictated everything, so I began to learn the substance and language of the law. I started dreaming about somehow finding a way to study it. I never mentioned that to anybody until one day, Mr. Kilborn suggested that I had a "feel for the law" and should seriously consider going to law school.

But it was just assumed that girls of my generation got married and then got pregnant, or got pregnant and then got married. Most of the students married each other. Almost none of my classmates, boys or girls, went to college. Getting pregnant was a common occurrence and a common fear among us. We knew what caused it, but we didn't have much information about how to avoid it, and none about what to do when it happened. Getting pregnant spelled the end of school. I definitely knew that I didn't want to get pregnant, and didn't want to get married, but I did want to finish school and after that, do something other than get married and get pregnant. What else was available?

In the summer of 1954, I enrolled in classes for an undergraduate degree, the first step in the journey which later enabled me to become the fifth woman in the entire three year law school population in 1957 at the University of Alabama. There were so few of us because women, especially in the South, had learned how to avoid rejection by not applying. I suspect that the few women who ventured into law or medicine or other fields, were actively encouraged to do so, or at least not overtly discouraged by their fathers in the field. Nelle Harper Lee, who was to write *To Kill a Mockingbird*, was among those who attended, although she didn't finish. One suspects that *Atticus* may have been inspired by her lawyer father.

I loved everything about the law. When the grades were posted, I think I made all A's in all subjects except one. None of the students were hostile at the start of the semester, but there was a marked difference in attitude after the grades came out. There was also a subtle, but discernible difference in the way the professors treated me. It seemed there was more eye contact, and maybe a less hostile demeanor.

Hostility may be too strong a word to express the sentiment that women were unlikely to ever be successful in the legal profession. That being so, why go through this? At least one professor suggested it was unfair for a woman to be there…because her very presence might have prevented a man from being admitted. The attitude of the faculty reflected recognition of the fact that the legal profession was not ready to welcome women to the ranks. The faculty was right about that.

I took turns being Number One in the class with Charles McPherson Audustin Rogers, III, or *Max* as I called him. We were neck and neck on our grades. He was assured a job with his father's law firm and I was assured no offer with any law firm regardless of my grades. So we agreed that Max would be Editor in Chief of the Law Review and I would be Associate Editor. We worked closely together for the next year or so. Being "law review" allowed us certain privileges, one of which was having coffee at Druid Drug Store where the legendary football Coach Paul "Bear" Bryant would go almost every morning. Max and I would time it so we would get there when he did. If he was alone, he would sit with us. Years later, at a cocktail reception, he would remember me as "someone that worked at Druid's."

During our last semester, major law firm representatives came to interview prospects and posted notices in the law school. One day, I was reading them when Dean Harrison, the best teacher I have ever had, came up beside me and quietly stated that I might not be included in that group. I knew it was painful for him to make that statement and he had done so only to spare me the embarrassment of being told by the interviewing firms. I appreciated his sensitivity and regretted being a part of his obvious discomfort.

However, it would never have occurred to me that I would be included in the invitation.

Upon completion of law school in August, 1959, and to my great surprise, Judge Robert Simpson, a senior member of the Alabama Supreme Court, offered me a job as his law clerk... a recommendation by Vince Kilborn, who was responsible for my having gone to law school in the first place. Judicial clerkships add great allure to one's job prospects, so my resume looked pretty good: first or second, I never was sure, in my class; an editor of the Law Review; and now a judicial clerkship. However, there was one characteristic I didn't have...I was not male.

Nevertheless, I began the search. More than one law firm senior partner told me I would make a remarkable legal secretary. Not one offered me a job as a lawyer. You didn't see any women where the money was, in the practice of law, or anywhere else.

Most didn't offer any reason and none was expected, but the most common one went something like this: "The members of this firm certainly have no bias against women, heck, the firm couldn't function without Ms. So and So, a secretary. She keeps the lawyers here functioning. We wouldn't know what to do without one or more of the secretaries, etc."

In the end, I opened an office as a sole practitioner in Selma. I had no money, of course. A representative of the Dallas County Bar Association welcomed me to town, but before he could invite me to join, the by-laws would have to be amended. Membership was then limited to white male lawyers. I stuck with this practice until it became clear that Selma was not the place for me. I made the judge and some of the lawyers uncomfortable by my presence. By this time, the race issue dominated every conversation. And I openly supported John F. Kennedy for president.

Prominent people in Selma joined the White Citizen's Council and I was asked to join. It was explained to me that the Council would not advocate violence, but would support the effort to stop integration. Something called the Sovereignty Commission was formed. Exactly what it did was not clear at the time, but it was later discovered that among the things it did was keep the names of white people who were suspected of supporting the black's efforts to change "our way of life." I am sure my name was among those kept by the Commission. My refusal to join the White Council was duly noted as well.

So I moved to Birmingham and found myself unable to get an appointment for an interview with any major law firm. They simply saw no need to waste my time or theirs.

I finally went to see the head of the Birmingham Bar Association, a well regarded man. I wanted his advice and I gave him my qualifications and asked him what he would suggest to me about finding a job. He mentioned the banks, the trust departments. I told him I wanted to save that for last, in case I couldn't find anything else. Then, he said, "Maybe the house counsel to some of the big corporations would hire you." Of course, he didn't suggest any of his firm's corporate clients and didn't offer to call any of them. But he offered for example, Vulcan Materials and Liberty National's legal departments. So I went to Vulcan Materials and met with one of the department head's assistants and told him Mr. Arant had suggested they might be interested in me. He was just stunned. He said, "Mr. Arant suggested you come here?" I said, "Well, not precisely here, but he suggested I devote my attention to legal departments of corporations that might hire me."

He said, "I just cannot understand that. We have truck drivers and workmen around and the language is such that it wouldn't be appropriate for a woman. It's just too crude for the tender ears of a female lawyer." I left without any promise of anything and of course didn't hear another word from them.

But it did lead me to Liberty National and I was incredibly hired…not as a real member of the legal department, but in the stock transfer department. They didn't assign me a proper office like the other lawyers…I sat in the same place as the secretaries and clerks. As time went on, I realized I had no future in terms of advancement and I wasn't treated like a real part of the legal department. I decided to change jobs for more of a challenge.

I went to Cumberland Law School to teach. They were looking for faculty they could afford on a real shoestring since it was a new operation. Of course, now, they are highly regarded all over America. I stayed nine years and it was a happy match. Somebody once said I taught enough law students to get myself elected when I ran for the state supreme court in 1972. The only people interested in the race were either judges or lawyers and I had taught almost all of them!

It *was* a real advantage, but I didn't win the first time I ran in 1972. I got in a runoff with a man who shared the same name as a well known political candidate who wasn't even *in* my race. Then, they put out negative flyers that said I was the wife of a prominent black civil rights lawyer, Arthur Shores, which I wasn't. I spent all my time trying to convince voters that *he* is not who he *claims* to be and *I* am not who he *says* I am! But I ran again in 1974 and that time, I won.

When I was running, a lot of the criticism came from women: "I don't know how on earth you can do that. I have all I can do keeping my children in carpools and taking them to all their activities. How can you have a career too?" They didn't have careers. Women didn't expect to work unless they had to. Men would say I shouldn't run and they truly believed it. It wasn't a put down to me…they thought it wasn't ladylike.

I took office in January 1975 and I was one among nine on the Supreme Court. All the rest of the justices were white men. By the nature of the function of an appellate court, the difference in treatment was extremely subtle and almost unconscious. For example, we would hold oral arguments and the courtroom would be filled with lawyers who had cases to argue. It was not uncommon, particularly for older lawyers, to address the court as "Your Honors," or "May it please the court," or any such introductory remark. But from time to time, they would say, "Your Honors and Mrs. Shores." It was as if their mind just didn't think I might be included in the expression of "Your Honors."

Usually, I didn't say anything, but once I did say, "Are you suggesting I am less honorable or is that an oversight?" I didn't match their mental image of what a judge is supposed to look like. If they had thought about it, they probably wouldn't have said it.

There were a lot of jokes, just casual chatter that was the same whenever a woman enters an all male team. I'm afraid my presence inhibited the spontaneity that existed. The feeling that you are inhibiting them does make you feel guilty.

I can say I worked harder than most of the others. Any woman trying to succeed in a man's world had very few mistakes to play with. One of the chief justices that I worked under observed that I didn't seem to use my law clerks much. I didn't work them as hard as some of the others. I suppose I wanted to make sure that I worked as hard, or harder. But after a couple of years, that went away.

I got into the swing of it.

Architecture & Engineering

LEATRICE B. MCKISSACK

Lea McKissack was selected from a pool of 105 nominees and presented with the National Female Entrepreneur of the Year award in 1990 by President George H. W. Bush for her role as the Chief Executive Officer of McKissack & McKissack, the oldest and largest African-American architectural firm in the U.S.

She went from math teacher to homemaker to corporate leader, expanding her company beyond the home base of Nashville to offices in Memphis, Montgomery, Washington, D.C., Philadelphia, and Manhattan. She has served as a member of the Federal Reserve Bank Board Advisory Council in Atlanta and has assisted governors and presidents through board appointments, forums and councils on subjects ranging from architecture to finance.

Her awards are numerous and include the SBA Small Business of the Year, the Premier Black Woman of Courage, the Human Relations Award, Business Woman of the Year, Howard University National Honoree School of Business, and a NAACP award recognizing companies over 50 years in business.

In 15 years, she took her husband's $15 million company to over $100 million with more than 400 employees. Her crowning jewel was the design contract for the National Civil Rights Museum in Memphis at the site of the Lorraine Motel where Dr. Martin Luther King, Jr. was assassinated. What began as a male firm for eight decades is today a firm headed by McKissack females. Lea's twin daughters Cheryl and Deryl took over when she decided to call it a day in 2001.

The Way I See It...

You have to do whatever comes to mind if you see you're not gaining any momentum. Keep fighting...keep knocking down the walls.

Papa, Here's Your Girl

My mother is the reason I am like I am.

I was the only girl in a family of five and she never made a distinction with my gender. Growing up with boys, I learned I was as good as they were. We all had the same responsibilities...washing dishes, cutting the grass. We called our mother the German General.

Maybe that is why I was able to run a company of all men. I didn't distinguish and still don't between a man and a woman.

I lived a very sheltered life. Married with children and retired from teaching at 39 due to my health, I took over running the household, money and all. My husband, Dee, didn't want me to do it, and it was hard to convince him to let me handle our money. Dee was the businessman. His father had founded McKissack & McKissack, and he was so very proud of it. We even had a park named after our family in Nashville...stained glass windows in our church too. His pride in the business was the main reason I decided not to sell it after his stroke.

I remember when it happened on May 9. I had flown to Washington, D. C. for our twin daughters' graduation from college. I sat with Cheryl as she called her father, and, lo and behold, he was making guttural sounds on the phone—a signal of a stroke or heart attack. In a panic, we called our doctor. About 40 minutes later, he called to tell me that Dee was in the hospital. I couldn't get home fast enough.

His prognosis was not good; the doctors advised me he would prob-ably never recover. The stroke had affected his brain. He was slightly paralyzed on his right side and his speech was slurred.

The very next morning at 7:30, my phone rang. The president of a large architectural firm wanted to speak to me. "Mrs. McKissack, we un-derstand your husband has had a stroke and we want to buy your com-pany."

Dazed and confused, Dee's recovery consumed my mind. I had given no thought to the business. "I don't have a clue as to what I'm going to do right now. Give me your name and let me get back with you."

Unbelievably, two other company presidents called me before 8:00 a.m.. I thought, "Here I am, devastated...my husband is lying near death in the hospital, and I don't know what I'm going to do." One minute I was going through my normal routine and the next minute, my whole life changed.

Finally, I thought I'd better get up out of bed and make some deci-sions. First, I needed to figure out how to keep this company. If they all wanted it that badly, I could run it myself!

The board of directors consisted of two vice presidents and Dee. The two vice presidents teamed up against my husband, outvoting him on numerous occasions. Dee traveled all the time bringing in the work while they moonlighted on the side, siphoning off the very work Dee was bringing in! Yet, they were still getting a big salary from the company. My husband was such a sweetheart, he wouldn't say anything about it. But I knew that the stress caused by this undermining and mismanagement contributed to his stroke.

First I called a lawyer, a friend of the family. He agreed that I needed to put my cards on the table. My decision was made. "I'm going into that office." On May 11, I walked into my husband's conference room for a stockholder's meeting with my lawyer on my right arm. They were ready for me. I sat at the front of the room with 5,000 or more shares, and em-ployees with only 25 shares given to them by my husband showed up with their lawyers! I couldn't believe they marched into my husband's office with their demands.

I made a statement. "I have high hopes my husband will be back. Un-til then, I will be running this company and I want to increase the board of directors." I voted myself onto the board, along with my three daughters. I also added an engineer and an architect, and subsequently hired them to come to Nashville and assess the company.

I realized my work was cut out for me—big time. I had stepped into a male world and none of them thought I could manage the business. They saw me as a female who could be manipulated and coerced to operate on their terms.

My oldest daughter, Andrea, moved home from Detroit and confronted me. "Get out of that bed 'cause I'm here to give you a quickie course in architecture and engineering and you are going to have to *get it.*" She resigned her engineering job and worked with me for three months, around the clock.

I never slept.

At night, I would brace myself with a quart of beer and sit down to read architectural contracts filled with difficult terms and technical language. When I woke up the next morning, the beer bottle would be empty and the contracts all over the bedroom floor. I would get up, get dressed and drive to the hospital to check on Dee, and then go to work. Often I would work all day long, nonstop, without food or breaks.

We had four companies: a construction company, a 216-unit apartment complex, an 86-unit apartment building and the architectural and engineering company. Nobody wanted to help my husband…they were all just taking. As soon as I caught them mishandling Dee's funds, I fired them.

As time went on, I whittled my husband's holdings down to just the architectural and engineering company. First, I sold the construction company because my husband had a total idiot running it. Dee knew he was a crazy man, spending his money foolishly.

The manager wouldn't work with me. He would hide financial information and company activity. Of course, he would give me money, thinking that would shut me up. Clearly, I couldn't run the company without information! I figured we had about 30 trucks flying around town with the McKissack name on them, presenting a huge liability to an owner who was kept in the dark. I was at a loss.

Every night I prayed and put it in God's hands, asking Him to help me with this one. I woke up at three in the morning and it came to me—I needed Dee's help. The next morning I set up a meeting with his friend and mentor, Hal Hardaway. I dressed Dee, helped him into his wheelchair and headed for the car. Hal owned a big construction company and had helped Dee get started. He had a tremendous influence over the manager running my construction company.

I pushed Dee, dressed in his best suit, into Hal's office and up to his desk. I sat down beside him ready to discuss the situation. I looked Hal in the eye and made my plea. "Hal, I need your help. My husband wants to sell the construction company, but I don't think I can approach the man who's running it. You have influence over him and I want you to try to help me do this."

Dee had been non-verbal since his stroke. As he tried to communicate with us, "Fine," was the only word that he could sound out. So his response to everything was, "Fine." Hal didn't know that the stroke had caused so much damage. He turned to my husband with a meaningful smile. "Dee, do you want to sell?"

Dee held his head up and answered firmly. "Fine."

Hal said, "Consider it done."

I made more money by making this move. I kept peace between the manager and myself. Eventually I sold the apartment complexes too, so I could concentrate on just the architectural and engineering business.

Going into my office was a trip to hell every day. I went in crying because the men were so mean to me. They just didn't want me there. I started on May 11 and by the end of July, I had fired every last one of my employees. I was treated badly—no one listened to my ideas or offered any respect. My husband's bookkeeper was mean as nails, and she was a female. They all worked in an environment that did not value women, and they were not about to let me change it. They would throw things at me across the office! One employee threw a pack of cigarettes at me. I looked at him in astonishment. "Have you lost your mind? I think you'd better get up and leave."

One of the vice presidents, who continued to siphon off money, patronized me, yet he didn't always follow through on his job. Due to his negligence in checking reports during the construction of a huge building at Tennessee State University, a wall fell down. The state of Tennessee called me on the carpet and sued my company. I paid $10,000 even with my liability insurance. Due to the negligence of employees, I had to solve one problem after another. It was awful.

The men in the company didn't want anyone to disagree with them, and the ones who didn't want to work for a woman left. They were determined to do it their way, ignoring the clients' wishes and mine. They wanted their money and didn't want to work for it. They didn't want to bother …it wasn't worth it to them. But it wasn't their money! I wouldn't stand for it. The customer is always right. The whole battle just wore me out.

In 1988, about one year after my firm was selected to design the National Civil Rights Museum, my husband died. I asked my daughters to join the firm. They were both professional engineers, trained from birth! This business was a family legacy: McKissacks had been running this company for eight decades. Our responsibility was to persevere.

The mayor appointed me to the Nashville Planning Commission composed of all white men except for the female chairman. I became the second black to ever serve. Due to my background and the way I was reared, I believed that I was just as good as anyone else. I always felt equal. I just didn't deal with color.

Sitting at the conference table, I felt like I wasn't there…they were totally ignoring me. A black physician, also a minister, asked the commission if he could use a high school parking lot for his Sunday parishioners. The commissioners declined with no discussion and moved on to the next topic. I stood up, took my papers and threw them the whole length of the table. Everybody stopped and asked, "What's the matter, Lea?"

I paused to make sure they all were listening. "Look, here's what's the matter. Number one, I didn't ask to be on this commission. The mayor appointed me…and since he did, I intend to do the best I can. Now can you tell me why this man can't use this parking lot?" They looked at me as if they were seeing me for the first time. They reconsidered and granted him use of the lot. From then on, everybody on the planning commission was my buddy, but it took me standing up and acting the fool to get their attention.

As a female, sometimes you act crazy in order to get your point across. You have to do whatever comes to your mind if you see you're not gaining momentum. So I did. I met with women's groups and delivered my message. "Keep fighting…keep knocking down the walls."

In 1989, I was the only black on the Cheekwood Fine Arts and Botanical Gardens Board in Nashville. I was solicited to sponsor Joe Williams, a popular singing artist who was performing a concert on the grounds. I thought long and hard about the statement my support would make. "That's a wonderful idea, but I don't know what kind of message it would send to the community, especially the *black* community, if I sponsor this event. Blacks, including myself, can't even attend the Swan Ball, our biggest fundraising benefit. If you want me to put money in this facility, you are going to have to open some doors for blacks."

It shocked them off their feet. In two days, they called. "Mrs. McKissack, your invitation is in the mail."

At the same time, I sat on the American Federation of Art Board housed in Manhattan and was bombarded with invitations to their events. I had even flown to New York and had dinner with the president of the board. Quite a difference in Nashville. I wasn't satisfied. "I'm not just concerned about me. I want other blacks there." It was the funniest thing. When I left that board, I had managed to open it up to everyone.

My family was active in the CME church in Nashville. The district Bishop sent me a first class ticket to Memphis to have lunch with the CFO of the national church from California. After our meal, the Bishop turned to me. "Please excuse me, Sister McKissack. I need to take a walk." Why had the Bishop gone to the trouble to fly me to Memphis only to leave the room when the meal was over? What kind of stunt were they trying to pull on me?

Suddenly I noticed an attractive young man at my elbow. He reached down in his briefcase and pulled out papers. "We thought it would be a great idea if you would take out a life insurance policy on yourself for a million dollars and leave it to Lane College."

I replied with my standard line, "Well, you know I never, ever do anything until I talk with my CPA." Abruptly, the Bishop reappeared and said it was time to go back to the airport. I was trying my best to hold back my astonishment. "It sure is!"

On the way to the airport, I talked to the Bishop. "Since you all want me to leave the college a million dollars, here's what you need to do for me—I want to go to the Dallas National Conference of Bishops to make a presentation. According to the history of my firm, I noticed that Moses McKissack, our founder, was the official architect of record for the CME Church."

Knowing this, the Bishop knew he had no choice but to grant my request. "Of course," he said.

Cheryl and Deryl met me in Dallas and we all attended the meeting. They stood behind me. We each wore white. I thanked the 16 bishops and told them about Moses, our founder. "Now," I said, "I want all of you to look at me real good and to look at these pretty daughters behind me. I want you to know one thing…it costs a lot of money for us to run multiple companies, make a living and look like this. And if I were to sign over a million dollar life insurance policy to you, my daughters would resurrect my body and tar and feather it. You need to get real busy—all of you around this table—and figure out how you can give our firm some architectural work. Then, when you need money, I won't mind writing you a $60,000 check to fix your roof. But it's not coming out of my pocket. We need to work together."

Only one took me up on my offer, the only one with any sense. I built a church for him in Atlanta. They would have never asked my husband to provide them with a life insurance policy. Because I was a woman, they thought they could strong arm me. It was always a fight.

People in business didn't know what to think of me. It was difficult to be a woman in a man's world, but I had the gumption to open my mouth and speak. I would not back down on what I knew to be right. I once heard someone ask, "Where did this feisty woman come from? Her husband was so nice!"

My career highlight occurred when my daughter invited me to meet with Dr. James Cheek, the President of Howard University in Washington, D.C. It was my daughter's intention to land a job for her employer, Turner Construction. I decided to tag along and for the first time, I realized that I had the power to make a difference. I learned that I had to demand the respect that I deserved.

When Dr. Cheek asked how he could help us, my daughter didn't say a word. So I stepped in and took over the conversation. "Dr. Cheek, I guess my husband would want me to establish a scholarship in his honor since he went here."

Suddenly I couldn't stop him from talking. He went on and on about who to contact and how to go about setting up the scholarship. In the midst of his current of words, I stopped him. "Wait a minute, why would I want to give you money to establish a scholarship when you have never given my company any business? My husband was educated and even honored at this school and all my children went here too."

He said, "You've never asked."

"I have been trying to get to you for the past three years. My company provides the services you need; yet, you have never considered utilizing our talents."

Amazed, he gave me his complete attention. "Who has stopped you from getting to me?" After I told him, he summarily fired the person and made me a promise. "You've got the next project." We ended up at his house for lunch and we stayed all the way through dinner and well into the night.

The next time I saw Dr. Cheek was aboard his yacht with his wife. We sailed for three days and when I walked off that yacht, my company had $50 million of work with Howard University.

I loved my father-in-law, Moses McKissack, or "Papa." He had six sons, but he always wanted a daughter. I can still hear him say, "I'd trade all six of these boys for just one girl." I wonder what he would say about his 60-year-old McKissack & McKissack Chief Executive Officer "girl" receiving an award from President Bush in 1990?

Papa, you sure got your girl!

Environmental

FAYE HELLER

*Faye Heller was in the trash business. Her path to freedom was
hauling and construction. Because she was a woman, she faced
problem after problem working in a male dominated industry. With
determination and sheer will, she achieved success and worked to
advance the status of women in all businesses.*

*She went to Beijing with Hillary Clinton for the Fourth World
Conference on Women and was appointed to the U.S. Small Business
Administration's National Advisory Council. She was on the national
board of NAWBO, National Association of Women Business Owners,
the NFIB, National Federation of Independent Businesses, and served
as President of Pennsylvania WIPP, Women Impacting Public Policy.
She was voted one of the top 50 women in business in Pennsylvania.*

*Faye's congressman presented her with the American flag flown
over the White House in her honor as the March of Dimes Woman of
the Year.*

*Her expert advice, ideas and opinions on small business issues
continue to promote and educate women everywhere.*

The Way I See It...

Women in non-traditional businesses were unheard of and still are. My industry was difficult to penetrate, but I managed.

Not Your Traditional Woman

My mother was a hard act to follow. A widow in the early 1960s, she decided to go into business with her brother. They opened one of the first one-hour dry cleaners, maybe even the first one. My mom, ambitious and very feisty, ran that business, always telling her brother and his wife what to do. Quite astounding, my mother.

When John F. Kennedy came to Pennsylvania, Congressman Bill Barron brought him to my mom's store for an introduction. Back then, as now, the choice of political party was Democrat, and she was very involved and influential. Some developers wanted to move her store to the other side of the street so they could build a parking lot. By the time my mom finished with them, they changed their minds and left her alone.

I was 11 when my father died. I had one sister. I grew up quickly, working through school to help support my family. I liked working, but the only objective for a young girl was to get married. By the time you graduated high school, you were supposed to have an engagement ring on your finger. My family picked out a husband for me when I was 17! It was arranged…a wedding shower, invitations, all of it. My mother thought this was normal and natural. Not me.

I told her I was not going through with the marriage—and I didn't. I thought I was way too young. It was ridiculous. I was apprehensive about the whole thing. I don't think I loved him … I don't think I knew what love was.

The girls I knew married as soon as they graduated high school. A few years later almost all of them had divorced. They went back to school after their divorce and then had a career, but they lost so much time. I was fortunate. I worked at night while I went to high school. When I graduated, I had a full time job at a fairly decent level with the government. That was remarkable.

Eventually, I married and had children. I wanted to continue my education and career, but my job was to stay home with my children. I had no one to watch them. Leaving your children with a babysitter was not an option. Absolutely no one did it. It was an awful time for any woman who wanted a career.

In the mid 1970s, after my children were older, I decided to go back into the business world. It was difficult. Even if you had a degree in business, you were offered a job as a secretary, an entry level position. I applied with an automotive distribution company, and when I took their aptitude test, they told me I was too intelligent for the secretarial position. They weren't sure if they could use me. I told them I was sorry about my level of intelligence, but I needed to work! So they hired me.

Once I understood how the business worked, I wanted to be promoted to outside sales. Because I did such a good job as secretary, they didn't want me to move. I needed to make more money and after several weeks of trying to convince them, they finally agreed to *inside* sales. My salary increased, but I knew that outside sales would be more profitable. I learned the business and covered my draw in the first couple of weeks. At that point, I started looking for another job.

I found a job in outside sales with another auto distributorship. Luckily, I was assigned some large commercial accounts. Several years passed with this company and I was doing well. My customers liked me and my salary steadily increased. Then, they told me they were bringing in a manager for my territory. I had worked so hard to establish that territory! I asked them to hire me for the position and they never responded. I couldn't believe it. I knew I needed to make another move.

I quit and started my own competing automotive and industrial distributorship business called Philly Fast. I offered my customers the same material, quality and price. They gave me their business! Ultimately, I saved my customers money. They liked my service better. I knew I was in a handicap position because plenty of men wanted my accounts, but I learned to listen. I knew clients liked to talk sports so I kept up with football and baseball games and scores.

It worked out well. I started the business in my home and it grew quickly—to the point where I had no space to eat. I used big spools of tubing as tables, but when the tractor trailers started pulling up, that's when I knew I had to move.

I expanded my business by establishing another company to manage hauling and construction. I managed to penetrate a difficult and unusual field for a woman. Of course, my mother was proud of me…she thought it was wonderful. On the other hand, some of my friends and family didn't understand. "What are you doing in this kind of business?" I told them I wanted to make more money and I knew how to do it this way. What could they say?

Some of the men I dealt with liked working with a woman instead of a man. That was the good part. But men in business, especially in construction and waste, absolutely did not like women in management positions. Even now, I would wager the big companies may have a small percentage of female employees, but they aren't managers. I remember one woman in charge of safety, Isabel. She did whatever they said. It looked good having her there, but she had no authority. Women worked only in lower management—at the weigh stations to hand out tickets and maybe in the office to do paperwork.

Women in non-traditional businesses were unheard of and still are. There's always a man, a husband, a brother or an uncle in the background. These are macho industries. When people asked me, "What do you do?" I told them that I was in the waste hauling business. They would look at me with a funny expression. "You don't look like you're in the waste hauling business."

"What does somebody look like in construction and hauling?"

"I don't know, but I didn't expect to see a woman."

Even officials made similar comments to me. After a while, it rolled off my back. I acquired the contracts, but I was definitely not one of the good 'ole boys. It was never easy to operate in a man's world. I never achieved what I could have if I had been a man. A typical network of men made sure that never happened. Middle management men saw me making money and the next thing I knew, they were trying to start their own companies and move me out. If I had been a man, that type of treatment would have never entered the equation.

Clients made passes at me but I usually straightened them out. It happened frequently, but I didn't think much about it. I was single and divorced then, and I had no interest in a relationship. Sometimes I would lose the account. I faced the worst situation with one of my large accounts. I had always dealt with one particular person at Levino Shipping Lines, a very large Greek company that managed the Philadelphia ports. He was replaced by someone that gave me a bad feeling.

One day, he asked me if I would be his girlfriend. Flabbergasted, I said no and told him that I thought he was married. He looked at me with a lack of respect. "Yeah, my wife is very sick." The next time I saw him, I expected more harassment and seriously considered wearing a wire. Sitting there in his chair, he threatened me. "If you don't go out to dinner with me, you're going to lose this account." The only way to handle this type of situation was to confront it. I called the office and the vice president held a meeting with all of us. The manager readily admitted what he did and the company did nothing about it. He was not reprimanded at all. I, of course, lost the account and it was a big one.

As far as finances were concerned, money was not available to a woman. Even today, whether it is state or federal money, mostly men receive the financing. Women that are starting out, especially in construction, find it almost impossible to get money. If they do receive financing, it's not enough to start a business or the rates are too high. Luckily for me, my situation was a little different. I had $20,000, a great deal of money back then, invested in my company when I started and could buy inventory. By the time I created my trucking company, I had established credit and was able to buy equipment.

The waste industry hasn't changed. They look for the easy way out. What they do is a sham. They hire people who don't really run the business but are somehow affiliated with that company. They use their name because they need contracts. There was plenty of Mafia in the business. I knew what was going on…in New Jersey and New York. I didn't want to get involved. My ethics meant more to me than money. I accomplished what I set out to do without compromising my principles.

When I certified for the city of Philadelphia and the Department of Transportation, they asked, "How can you run a trucking company if you don't know how to drive a tractor trailer?"

I looked at them in disbelief. "Are you telling me that all these large trucking companies across the United States are run by men that know how to drive a rig? What difference does it make if I can drive or not? I know the regulations. I know what has to be done. I know about my equipment." The second class treatment women received infuriated me.

Non-traditional women business owners still have to put up with this type of aggravation. I can't believe in this day and age, women are still pushed back and undermined by so many who could help.

You just have to get out there, sell your product and grow your business. After a while, you realize that others do understand you and respect your accomplishments. Your opinions matter and you can make a difference.

My struggles were staggering at times, but I persevered. Both of my children were in the business with me until my son became ill. He was misdiagnosed with a virus and died 24 hours later. It was strep pneumonia. At the time, he was thriving in the company, doing incredibly well. It broke my heart. Some days, it was hard to carry on. But of course, I did.

I have learned valuable lessons...overcoming obstacles, establishing relationships, penetrating unknown fields, and paving new ground. When I retired, I decided to use my knowledge and experience to assist others pursuing their dreams in business. My pro-bono work with women and my political volunteer work fulfill my days...aiding, counseling, assisting and protecting the interests of small business.

Writer

MARTHA BOLTON

Martha Bolton was a staff writer for the legendary comedian Bob Hope for over 15 years. She has written comedy for such performers as Phyllis Diller, Ann Jillian, Jeff Allen, Mark Lowry, Fritz Coleman and more. She also wrote for both Bob Hope's and Wayne Newton's military shows for the troops.

She is a speaker and author of over 50 books, ranging from children's entertainment to youth devotionals, musicals, comedy essays, and dramatic sketches about marriage, family and relationships. Martha is also the "Cafeteria Lady" for Brio *magazine.*

The winner of four Angel Awards, she received an Emmy nomination for Outstanding Achievement in Music and Lyrics, and a Dove award nomination for A Lamb's Tale, *a children's musical. From Media Fellowship International, she received the Ambassador Award.*

In Bob Hope's words, "Martha Bolton finds fun in the familiar, the mirth in the mundane, the belly laughs in the bellyaches of everyday living."

According to Phyllis Diller, Bolton is one of the funniest writers alive today.

The Way I See It...

We don't know all the why's of life. But good things happen when you trust God and don't give up Hope!

Touched by Hope

I never dreamed I would be a professional writer.

I loved to write, and in fact, I wrote my first book when I was nine years old. It was called *No Fun Being Young*, and it was about growing up as the youngest of five children in our family.

By the age of 12, I was writing poetry. I would tape my typed poems on the wall above my bed. There were about 30 of them. I told my mother it was cheaper than wallpaper.

At 14, I entered a gag-writing contest, and my gag was one of the winners printed in the paper.

I wrote my first play, produced by my church, when I was 21 years old.

It wasn't until I sold my first magazine article at 23 years old that I realized you could get *paid* to write. I just assumed it would always be a hobby for me. I never thought it could become a career.

I had briefly considered becoming a professional ice-skater, and might have went in that direction had it not been for the failed execution of a double loop spin. My teacher probably would have been more understanding had I done it on the ice, but it was after losing my balance in the snack bar, and thus my life went in a completely different and unexpected direction (much like my legs did that day).

I took secretarial courses in high school, and landed a job at an insurance company, and then, as a church secretary. I figured that was what I was supposed to do with my life.

But I never stopped writing. As church secretary, I started "roasting" the pastor at banquets. Hearing the laughter of the people, as well as the pastor, was something that I loved.

I took their laughter as encouragement and began submitting material to various comedians. It took a year to hear back from the first comedian. I don't know if it took her that long to *get* the joke, but she bought, and continued buying over the years. One of my first regular clients for jokes was Phyllis Diller. We had the same philosophy on housekeeping and cooking. I can't cook. For years, my family thought mold was a frosting!

I wanted to get into television script writing. After much encouragement from Gene Perret, the creative consultant on *Mama's Family*, I wrote a couple of spec scripts for the show. The producer liked my work and said he would be calling me in for a pitch session the following season. Unfortunately, the show got cancelled before that could happen.

Gene, however, was also a writer for Bob Hope, and recommended me to Bob. I tried out; Bob liked my writing, and ended up hiring me as his first woman staff writer. I was on the Bob Hope writing staff, writing television specials, personal appearance material, tributes, song parodies, and whatever else he could think of until he retired—about 15 years in all.

My best advice to someone aspiring to follow their dreams is never give up. There will always be rejection—people who don't believe you can do it—people who try to stop you. But don't give up.

My favorite "don't give up" story happened at Bob Hope's 90th birthday party that his wife Dolores gave him in their backyard. Their guest list included legendary celebrities and two presidents, Gerald Ford and Ronald Reagan. I had an opportunity to chat briefly with President Gerald Ford. After he walked away I regretted immediately that I had not gotten my picture taken with him. This made me all the more determined to get my picture taken with President Ronald Reagan. I told my husband that I was going to try to get close to him. "If it looks like we're talking," I said, "snap the picture!" Unfortunately, I couldn't get close to him until they gave the call for dinner. As everyone made their way toward the dinner tent, I noticed I was walking right behind Ronald Reagan. This was my chance! I picked up my pace a bit and caught up with him. Normally I don't do this sort of thing, but I gathered up my courage and asked the President if he would mind if my husband took our picture. He graciously said, "Not at all." The sun had set, and it was starting to get rather dark—but no worries—the camera had a flash. The President and I posed for the shot. We smiled. My husband took the picture. But the flash didn't go off. My heart sank. The President asked if I wanted to try again. So we posed, smiled one more time and my husband took the picture. The flash still didn't go off. I thanked the President and we all went to dinner.

The next day, I rushed the film to the development center and hoped and prayed that something turned out. I was heartsick to see that nothing showed up. It was just a black square. To make myself feel better, I enlarged that black square and hung it on my wall because *I* know it's me and Ronald Reagan!

The topper to that story happened one night at a banquet where I was speaking. I shared the tale with the audience. After my speech, a man approached me and asked if I ever got my picture. I laughed and said, "No, I had my two chances and I blew it."

"Well, maybe I can help," he said. He pulled a card from his pocket and handed it to me. It was Michael Reagan, the President's son. That next week, I got a call from the President's office inviting me and my entire family to have our picture taken with him. The photographer took a picture of *me* with him, my *husband* with him, each one of my *sons* with him, and one of *all* of us together. It turned out much better than any photo my little camera would have given me.

Another "don't give up story" taught me long ago to have faith when we can't see the big picture of life's challenges. I married my husband when I was 18 years old. Within the first year, I got pregnant. Sadly, that pregnancy ended in a miscarriage. I waited the recommended time and got pregnant again. I made it to the fourth month, the fifth month and the sixth. I made it all the way to one week before my due date. During my routine visit with my OB-GYN, he couldn't find a heart beat. After some stressful scheduling issues due to the doctor's international trip plans, I was finally told to come to the hospital to be induced. Our ten-pound-two-ounce son was stillborn.

Life can sure bring us some disappointments, can't it?

My husband and I began applying for adoption. The wait was long. It was also heartbreaking to walk by an empty and very quiet nursery, day after day. So we decided to move to a different house…a change of scenery might do us good. We sold our two-bedroom home and bought a four-bedroom home. Some people couldn't understand why we needed such a large house, but we had faith that God was going to give us a family one day.

The week we moved was stressful. We called several adoption agencies to tell them of our new address, but because we had moved to a different county, we would be dropped from their list. We would have to reapply in our new county, which meant going back to square one. We were heartsick. Our step of faith seemed to be backfiring.

Our church was having special services that week and my husband asked if I wanted to go. I told him no. I didn't want to hear some preacher tell me how much God loved me because I wasn't feeling it very much that night. We stayed home and put one of the rooms together. The nursery seemed the easiest. My husband helped me until around midnight, and then went on to bed because he had to get up early the next morning. That was fine, because between midnight and two o'clock in the morning, I had one major pity party for myself. It wasn't fair. Why did we have to go through all this pain? Finally, at two o'clock I gave it up. I told God that I still didn't understand it, but I was going to trust Him. He had a plan, and it would be a good plan, and then I went to bed. At six o'clock in the morning, the phone rang. It was an out-of-state adoption agency telling me they had a baby boy for us.

Within the next two years, we adopted another son, and I was six months pregnant when we adopted him! With three sons, every bedroom of that four-bedroom home was filled.

Never give up hope!

Media Health

DR. JUDY KURIANSKY

Judy Kuriansky, Ph.D., known as "Dr. Judy" by her millions of fans is an internationally known radio and TV personality, clinical psychologist and certified sex therapist, popular lecturer, columnist and author. An adjunct in the Department of Clinical Psychology at Columbia University Teachers College and in the Department of Psychiatry at Columbia Medical Center, she is also a visiting professor of China's Peking University Health Science Center and the director of Psychosocial programs for U.S. Doctors for Africa. An expert on relationships, AIDS, peace-building and other topics, she is a United Nations NGO representative for two international organizations, who has healed people's interpersonal relationships. She also assisted survivors of disasters after 9/11, the Asian tsunami, SARS in China, bombings in Israel, and earthquakes around the world.

This bridging individual and inter-cultural work is evident in her 12 books with topics ranging from The Complete Idiots Guide to Healthy Relationships *to* Beyond Bullets and Bombs: Grassroots Peacebuilding between Israelis and Palestinians.

A columnist for the New York Daily News *and* China Trends Health *magazine, she has been interviewed and featured in newspapers around the world, from the* New York Times *to the* International Herald Tribune. *Winner of the first International Outreach Award from the American Women in Radio and TV, she has hosted radio call-in advice shows for over 22 years and is a frequent commentator on* CNN *on* Showbiz Tonight and Issues with Jane Velez Mitchell.

A high achiever, Dr. Judy has touched many people's lives and taken many risks to chart a unique life journey.

The Way I See It...

Do what you love—that is your purpose in life.

Spreading Peace

When I was eight years old, my mother asked me, "What do you want to be when you grow up?" At the time, my response was not, "a sex therapist!" No one knew that field existed back then. I didn't even answer "a psychologist," a profession I love. My mother has reminded me of my answer, "I want to do something for world peace." Whatever caused me to say that certainly set the tone for my life's path.

During my childhood, my father always encouraged me to take risks, to be bold and adventuresome. I remember going to California with him and we bought a map of the stars' homes and drove around to see them. On an impulse, when we were in front of Tony Curtis' home, he said, "Go out and say hello and say how much you like his movies." I did! I was so impressed that Mr. Curtis gave me his picture and signed it. I kept that photo on my desk for years.

Another defining experience happened when I was eight years old. My father and I were driving in the hills of Kentucky where we lived. We got lost and I started to cry that we would never see our family again. My dad said, "Judy, don't cry. We're not lost. We're on an adventure." That reassurance taught me the importance of feeling safe, no matter what, and of embracing adventure. Now, in my career, I help others feel safe, especially after disasters, and I continue to see every experience as an adventure.

My mom deserves credit too. Like an angel with a heart of gold, she taught me about having a kind heart, love and empathy. Her devotion to me is unending. She listens to all my radio shows and keeps every newspaper clipping about me. She especially cherishes the *In Touch* magazine article where I give advice to President Obama and his wife for a happy relationship. I value my mother's advice: "Always trust everything you say and do. You have worked so hard and know so much. Trust your judgment and feel pride and pleasure in your accomplishments." Granted, she may have been a bit Pollyanna with my brother, sister and I...as if everything will work out for the best and everyone has good intentions.

My career has mixed my profession of clinical psychology with media, including television, radio, magazines, newspapers, and new media. Basically, I am a "media psychologist." While I see patients privately in an office like a traditional therapist, I also discuss psychological issues and give advice in public venues. I've been a pioneer in this field.

People often ask me how I discovered such a path. My mother wanted me to be a French teacher and my father wanted me to go into computers—which was very prescient of him to suggest this in the 1950s. I considered those subjects, and majored in math in college for a while and even got an A+ in advanced trigonometry. I also studied French in Switzerland and read Descartes and Beckett in French. But I wanted to work with people, so psychology presented a perfect field...unraveling the mystery of the mind and of people's behavior...figuring out why people do what they do.

Getting into the field of sexology was serendipitous. At the very beginning of the academic field of sexology, I was a *just-out-of-college* research scientist working with a group of psychiatrists at Columbia Medical School who were asked by the famous sex researchers, Masters and Johnson, to evaluate their treatment methods—essentially the first notable American "sex therapy." I found it encouraging to see how people's lives could become happier with such a short intervention in this area of life. Asked to present my research on television concerning topics like depression and anxiety, producers found out I knew about sex and they started asking me to talk more publicly about that topic. The interest was clearly there. I was hired by a local ABC television station as a feature reporter and then asked to host a call-in radio advice show. I agreed, and went on the air answering questions five nights a week, three hours a night.

Being a psychologist came naturally—working out the puzzles of people—and the broadcasting aspect of my career also evolved naturally, an especial blessing, considering that I was starting in a "top market" like New York. But it was not always easy being a sex therapist in the early years. There was controversy, especially from religious groups, about "sex talk on the air" and I went through some painful experiences and tough criticism that were hard to face and talk about. At the time, sex was still somewhat taboo. Dr. Ruth, the famous sex educator who started broadcasting at the same time, was more easily accepted because she was a grandmother figure. She also had an unmistakable German accent that people liked to imitate—especially her famous sayings "have good sex" and "use contraceptives."

Criticism came from groups affiliated with the arch conservative religious right. A Senator wrote opinion pieces in the Atlanta newspaper protesting our show. Yet, we were exceptionally popular. To this day, young people tell me they listened through earphones under the covers and talked about the calls at school the next day. They still thank me for helping them feel better about themselves and helping them find healthy relationships and learn about self esteem and sex. My heart sings, as they are so successful and such nice people. I am honored to be part of their development.

Another trying time was when a group of Philadelphia parents picketed one of our stations airing the show, trying to get it off the air and get me in trouble with my profession. In a TV debate, which I accepted, one of the parents accused me of child abuse. I was hurt and shocked. Because so many youngsters are abused—physically, emotionally and sexually—the show helped them talk about their experiences and get help. Our massive young listener audience knew that. Our ratings were remarkably high—enough to be syndicated all over the country and even to Japan.

Experiences like that were painful to me since I don't like controversy. I like to be liked and do things people like and want. I lost sleep. I was depressed. I questioned myself. I sought support from family and friends. The attacks seemed unfair. The critics considered the content morally wrong—corrupting youth. But everything we experienced on the air reaffirmed the opposite—listeners and fans found it empowering, uplifting, valuable and responsible. We were serious but never judgmental. We respected everyone. The audience was Hispanic, Latino, Asian, Black, White, rich, poor and everything in between. They needed to talk to someone and enjoyed both the education and the entertainment. Fortunately the criticism was balanced with such listener appreciation. Youngsters would tell me, "Dr. Judy, you changed my life," or "I don't know what I would have done without you," or "You taught me to love myself." I understood why; I never thought I was talking about sex, per se. It was more about self-love and healthy relationships. The listeners realized that.

Over the years, thousands of people asked me how to make their lives happier and more fulfilling...emotionally and sexually. It has been very satisfying—and touching—to help people express feelings and work through the important and private parts of life they can't easily talk to anyone else about. The reason my radio, TV, and magazine audiences have grown so large is that people need a public outlet and someone they trust to talk to. Talking about such sensitive subjects publicly was challenging. It was so new and controversial. It took a great deal of courage.

Fortunately, a lot of people wanted me to continue what I was doing. In the end, I believe God put me in that role for very specific reasons. It must have been God because it certainly wasn't my plan. I had started out helping people with disorders like schizophrenia and depression and ended up being an on-air sex therapist and psychologist. Somebody's hand was in that besides mine, guiding me to say the right things to uplift and help others.

Ultimately, I expanded from helping people find inner peace in their relationships to facilitating a more global peace—essentially going from the microcosm to the macrocosm. I have spent many years as a citizen ambassador for peace in the world. I have been called a "bridge of peace" by government officials in China. I have worked in disaster relief all over the world, writing books about resolving conflict, and representing two international NGOs at the United Nations.

After many years, I'm finally at peace with what I do. I've brought together all the aspects of my interests and dreams. I played in an all-woman's band in the 1970s just for fun. Now I co-produce and perform in a peace anthem band, called the *Stand Up for Peace Project*. We have played original peace anthems at an international summit against nuclear war in Hiroshima, and for Peace Laureates like the Dalai Lama and Reverend Desmond

Tutu. The Dalai Lama crossed the stage and held our hands and said, "Very powerful." I was once afraid to tell people I played music in a band, for fear they would not find it respectable. Accepting myself now, I have found a way to harness my music to the goal of peace in the world.

If there is anything I still need to work on, it is to stop driving myself too hard. I want to accomplish too much in too little time. I want to experience all life has to offer. I climbed the Himalayas and scuba dove in Australia. There is so much to savor, too much to do! I only sleep five hours a night at the most. This pressure has increased as I get older and become more aware of mortality. People occasionally accuse me of being a workaholic. At times, I get upset when they say, "Something is wrong that you cannot just do nothing." Since I feel fully in control of whatever I choose to do and enjoy it all, I hardly take a day off from "accomplishing something." I have resolved that I am a playaholic, different from others who want time off. I rarely just "vacation." For example, on a trip to American Samoa with my husband and his sister, we met a woman who was running for office. She revealed to us for the first time that she had been abused. The next day, we put together a live TV show about domestic violence to alert the island to this problem. It became part of her platform for reform. It was work, but it was satisfying to know we made a major contribution to the culture. Such creative and useful projects give me ultimate happiness.

I also love coming up with new ways to approach issues. I developed the three R's for young people to remember: Respect, for yourself and others; Responsibility; and the Right, to say yes or no. I encourage people to "love yourself for who you are...go for what you want and ignore naysayers because they are just expressing their own fears."

This is a new world...of opportunity for all to embrace diversity. I have long been interested in diversity...of ideas and cultures...and it is especially wonderful to be teaching at Columbia, where my students come from every country: Portugal, Israel, Nigeria, Mexico, India, Germany, Norway, Bulgaria and Russia. I have been inspired to go to many of those countries to do something useful for people living there. I've studied Brain Theory, Shamanism and Buddhism in Nepal, and Tantra, all of which are major transitions and influences for my work and outlook. As a result, I have created new programs integrating western and eastern philosophies and traditions. My commitment for inter-cultural peace has manifested in many ways, including editing two books about the Israeli-Palestinian crisis.

I feel blessed to create my own life every day now. I don't do things that I *have* to do. I spend a lot of time in volunteer work—living like Bill Gates, without his huge billions! I am happy and satisfied with "who I am, where I am and what I am doing."

One big regret I have is while my brilliant, wonderful husband Edward and I had magical experiences together at home and all over the world, we both worked so many hours that we drifted into our own worlds. Facing regrets, I tell myself that I have to accept responsibility and mistakes, and believe in a higher destiny. I also regret not having children, but I find strength in working with millions of kids and with selected students who feel like my kids.

My childhood was blessed with a happy family and school successes—receiving a "medal of excellence" in junior high and being voted "most popular girl" in high school, but tragedy befell when my father and my brother died. I felt helpless to save them. I was devastated when some people made comments about my brother's death. "He has this famous sister, a psychologist. She should have made everything better." I had to resolve that I couldn't.

In darker moments, I am inspired by Robert Schuller's phrases, "turn scars into stars" and "turn problems into possibilities." Another inspiration is the title of a book, *Feel the Fear and Do It Anyway.* I am mindful of one of my childhood favorite books: *Le Petit Prince* by St. Exupery. Country music singer/songwriter John Denver gave me a copy of that book. It is about a young boy stranded in the desert who meets an E.T.-like prince and truisms emerge, like "everything is perfect in the best of all possible worlds." I try to reconcile this with being a humanist and also having an existential view questioning the meaning of life and making sense of choices one makes.

My advice to others is the same I give myself: realize your dreams without letting fears of money or people or other circumstances block your fulfillment. I wish the world's values would change, since many people care more about money and rewarding celebrity than they do about heart, commitment and loyalty, and valuing medical research.

My other guiding principles: Be strong and ask for what you need and want. Be confident that you are special and have something unique to contribute. If something doesn't work out, then it wasn't meant to be and may even have saved you from a potential disaster. Put your energy where you are embraced. I believe *what your mind can conceive, you can achieve.* I like the similar phrase, *where thought goes, energy flows and manifestation grows.*

Production

"What is sad for women of my generation is that they weren't supposed to work if they had families. What were they going to do when the children were grown? Watch the raindrops coming down the windowpane?"

—Jacqueline Kennedy Onassis
(1929–1994) America's former First Lady

JEANNE HARRISON

Before television became popular, Jeanne Harrison won two Emmys for two huge radio series she produced and directed. She delivered the Cisco Kid *and* Boston Blackie, *along with many musicals and all the big band half-hour shows. She was the first woman to produce a coast to coast television show called* Yesterday's News Reel.

Famous in show business, she was the first woman in The Friars Club and has appeared in eight books, including The Ad Game *by Judith Katz. She was also a member of the Director's Guild.*

After working for large corporate producers, she formed her own company, Harrison Productions, in 1971 in New York City. As producer and director, her clients included Alcoa, Bloomingdales, General Foods, Colgate-Palmolive, Procter & Gamble and Texaco. Her work received such major awards as the Clio, the Monitor and the Peabody.

In following her family's footsteps, Jeanne pioneered her way into show business at an early age, leaving a trail for her two daughters, Liza and Lydia, to follow.

Author's Note: Ms. Harrison passed away after her interview and before the publication of this book.

The Way I See It...

If I found myself in a bad situation, there was only one way to fix it. Get help and go along with whatever was necessary. You have to be open. You can't be closed all the time, doing hidden things.

I Cried, I Smiled

I come from a show biz family. My mother was Henrietta Harrison, the manager of WCAU, a huge radio station in Philadelphia. The first woman to produce a radio show, *The Eddie Cantor Show*, she also started the highly successful and well-known national women's club, *Women in Radio and Television*. An influential lady, she sat on many boards and served as head of *The American Society for the Prevention of Cruelty to Animals*.

Because my mother was a powerful media executive, I had the rare privilege to accompany her to the studio when I was young. I acquired a real taste for it. Eventually, I decided to get into the business too. I wanted to "put on plays in radio." To get my foot in the door, my mother found a job for me in the typing pool at NBC typing scripts. I lasted maybe 10 minutes! I just couldn't do it. It was ridiculous to type scripts.

The next day, I submitted an application to Ziv, a production company later bought out by United Artists. John Sinn interviewed me and we talked quite a while. A few days later, I received a card in the mail notifying me that I had been selected for the job. Over 5,000 people applied for that job, and they chose me. I didn't understand why. Many years later, after we had worked closely together, I asked John why he hired me. "Many people who applied were much more qualified than I was. Why me?"

He said, "Because your eyes were honest."

I thought to myself, "How silly, if that's what your qualifications have to be." Right off the bat, I could see that being a woman would present many challenges in a male dominated field.

Recording all the big bands for the half hour shows was one of my job responsibilities with Ziv. I went to California to record Freddy Martin's band. The first day, I sat alone in the studio control room. The engineer hadn't arrived yet. All of a sudden, in a flurry, a group of men came in and stole a gorgeous Steinway piano ... right off the stage! Dressed like movers, they casually strolled in and rolled out the piano. They saw me sitting there, but they walked right past me. "She's five foot and a half, what's she gonna do?" Men have a lot more nerve than women.

One of the members of the Lombardo's band, Carmen, cried all the time like a baby. His band would send him in the control room where I worked until he could compose himself. The engineer would step out, and Carmen would call his mother. He didn't even notice that I was in the room. I didn't exist to him because I was a woman.

I was right there at the start of the telly—or television. It was wonderful. I did the first cross country television show, *Yesterday's News Reel*—all the big disasters, elections, and news—a big deal for a woman back then. They made me head producer and gave me over 250,000 feet of reels they had purchased. I started to make news shows with it. Nobody asked me about it and nobody ever told me what to do.

As time went on, I wanted to do "real live work." I grabbed the opportunity to direct and produce television commercials for J. Walter Thompson Advertising Agency, the largest agency in the United States. I worked for seven years as executive producer with direct product control over Listerine, Lever Brothers products, Standard Brands and others. As head of production, I used my creative side.

I was young, but somehow I grasped the idea that if I smiled when I asked someone to do something, it usually worked. It was tough working in a man's field. We mustn't forget that back then women in the workplace had no clear directives—no one had come before them to pave the way.

Men lorded over female employees. They thought women's ideas could be squashed. Women were blamed for all the wrong reasons. If you tried to defend yourself, management would call you petty. One time, I refused to use one of our art director's campaigns because I thought it was inept and missed the mark. He told our group that he wouldn't work with me anymore because if he created something, I wouldn't use it. He missed the whole point. I did work with him, just the same, but the situation was stupid. *He* was stupid. It was a constant battle, and men didn't want women to win at anything.

One of the writers, a female friend, asked me to help her with a spot. We worked all morning and then headed to the commissary to eat lunch. We had an hour, but she needed to finish her drink, so I went back to work. About 30 minutes later, a man came to give me a message. "You'd better go to the ladies room and get your lady." She was drunk.

I had the head of the studio hold the back elevator so I could take her to her driver. I didn't want anybody to know her condition. I remember him shrugging it off. "What's the difference? Nobody will even miss her. She's not important." You see, men felt so much bigger than you. Even if they didn't do anything to you, you knew they were going to step on you. You knew that from the very beginning.

The advertising agency wanted to revive the product, Rinso. I devised an idea to show laundry in black light, and sure enough, the laundry looked good enough to eat. The lighting emphasized the colors and whites. I wanted to put sunglasses in the box for the consumers. The laundry would be so bright that they would need sunglasses. Lever Brothers liked the idea and decided to give $8 million to the agency to develop the concept. One of the research people, a young guy really full of himself, said it wouldn't work. "Oh, we can't let it go like this. If a woman opens this box and sees a pair of dark sunglasses, she'll think that the Rinso is dangerous and may hurt her if she uses it." That young man was head of research and he lost the $8 million account for J. Walter.

Tradition was important at the agency. If you wanted to have lunch at your desk, a maid would come down from the kitchen, donning a hat and an apron, with food on a tray to serve you. Those were the days! But those days would come to an end for me when I landed the "big one." I received an inquiry from the head of American Home Products, a huge company. A buddy of mine had moved over there and recruited me. Essentially, they wanted me to start a company within their company. I jumped at the chance. I was in charge of radio and television production, serving as senior vice president and creative director for their in-house advertising agency.

After a short time, I knew that something wasn't right. The head of my division was a very strange man. Whatever I suggested, he would do. One day, he asked me to lunch and made a sexual proposition. I said absolutely no. I wouldn't even consider it. I was married with a family. That afternoon, an executive vice president appeared at my office and let me go—the only time I have been fired. I held the position of vice president and this happened at the height of women reporting their bosses for harassment, but I didn't make a fuss. If they wanted to fire me, I certainly didn't want to work for them. I deserved a red rose for that decision. I certainly had to swallow a lot in those days.

I had the experience and the know-how, so I decided to start my own company, Harrison Productions. In the beginning, most people, even women, treated me negatively. In all the years of my business, I only received three big jobs from women. Women enjoyed hiring companies run by men because men took them to *21* or other great restaurants and theatres. I entertained clients, too, but that shouldn't have been the *reason* to hire me.

About five years after I started my company, the same man who propositioned me at American Home Products called me. "I don't know whether you want to talk to me or not, but I'd like you and your company to work for me." He had his own agency, so I took the job. He was present at every shoot. He never touched me or was inappropriate. Never referred to the earlier situation, nothing. I never said anything either. What was the point? Years had passed and he insinuated that he had changed. He didn't bother me, and I didn't bother him.

The Friars Club had been all male for over a hundred years. Women could only go if they were attached to a man in some way…either married or as a guest. I went to the club frequently. People would invite me and I would see old friends.

Women were becoming more and more visible as employees and leaders throughout the world and public pressure decreed that a man's club was archaic. The club knew they would have to make a token gesture. They interviewed me and let me know what I should expect if I were given membership. "You have to be careful here. It's all men and you have to go along with what we do." The front page of the *New York Times* reported the story, a charming little piece about a woman given membership to the Friars Club.

My second banana, as we called our assistants, was a darling, talented and affable boy named Bill that worked at J. Walter Thompson Advertising agency with me. When I left the agency, he left with me. We were together for over 25 years. Working in New York, Bill and I discovered that the unions ruled with an iron fist. We had a job for a refrigerator freshness powder with a full crew on a stage at the Bowery. The union had hired two deputies on the crew to report any "illegal activity" to the union boss.

Unexpectedly one day, Bill, almost in tears, ran into my office. "What are we going to do? They've reported the shoot back to the union! They can stop the shoot and then we're in for thousands of dollars." Apparently we had broken some rules.

Within an hour, a limo pulled up outside the building. Two men from the union climbed out. Bill, nervous and crying, stood next to me. I didn't know what to do. I had never dealt with the unions, and they had reputations as tough goons. We put the two men in a back room until I decided how to tackle the problem: cry. Yes, that's it, cry! The goons assured me that whatever I had to do was my call and not to worry about a thing. All the bad things about the shoot just disappeared!

When that happened to me, a whole new world opened up. What an experience! I realized how powerful I could be, when and if I wanted to be.

According to some industry insiders today, there are too many women in show business and not enough men. Everything has changed. Negativity is floating around, especially with regards to women. Women are doing it to themselves. They are afraid they won't receive the recognition that they deserve.

In my day, moving around in a man's world was not easy. I didn't scream and make demands. I figured out an easier way to do it. I did it with smiles. Believe me, I wasn't *happy*. I just *looked* happy. It sounds ridiculous, but it's true. I don't mean that I gave myself away. I didn't. And if I found myself in a bad situation, there was only one way to get out of it. Get help and go along with whatever was necessary. You have to be open. You can't be closed all the time, doing hidden things.

Finally, I truly believe in humor. How could it ever work between a man and a woman if it weren't for humor? If companies like American Home Products recognized the humor in life and did not take themselves too seriously, they would receive much more from their people. Humor certainly lightens the load.

"Success is having a flair for the thing that you are doing, knowing that it is not enough, that you have got to have hard work and a sense of purpose."

—Margaret Thatcher
Retired British politician

BARBARA DURY

Best known for her work as a producer for the television show 60 Minutes, *Barbara Dury has seized opportunity and had the extraordinary vision to achieve a highly successful career in communications. She credits her parents for her tenacious ability and determination to persevere...to keep moving forward.*

From a small job at a radio station in San Francisco, she climbed her way to the top echelon of television production, winning an Emmy and an American Women in Radio and Television Award, and sharing the Alfred I. DuPont-Columbia University Award.

She has worked with seminal figures in broadcasting such as Mike Wallace, Lesley Stahl, Morley Safer, Ed Bradley and Steve Kroft and skillfully interviewed top celebrities and international political figures such as Ronald Reagan, Bill and Hillary Clinton, Gerald Ford, Jimmy Carter, Joseph Biden, Orrin Hatch, Benjamin Netanyahu, Kevin Spacey, Larry King, Michael Caine, Liza Minnelli, Julie Andrews and countless other luminaries.

She researched, reported and produced over 100 segments for 60 Minutes, 60 Minutes II *and* The 20th Century with Mike Wallace *on wide-ranging subjects from John Paul II to airport security, from profiles of extraordinary women and media personalities to news stories such as the Challenger disaster and the perils of whistle blowing.*

In her usual manner of "moving on," she found herself on the launch team for the first independent television news station and Web TV channel in Amman, Jordan, and the first investigative reporting center in Dhaka, Bangladesh, contributing extensively to these sweeping endeavors.

The Way I See It...

You may not find out what your career will be until way down the road. It just evolves. Once you've gotten there, stick to it. There are always days when you wonder if it is worth it, but it is...in the end.

Moving Forward

I started working in radio, but quickly realized I was fascinated with the whole medium of television. When I left the radio station where I was working as an assistant, my co-workers asked me what I was going to do when I returned to my home state of New York. For some reason, I told them I was going to work at *60 Minutes*. They said, "Yeah, right!"

When I arrived in New York, it was definitely crunch time...I needed to get a job. Through a friend of a friend, I interviewed at CBS and ended up working as a clerical assistant in an accounting department. I was willing to take any job I could find at the main headquarters. One day, I decided to randomly call the personnel department. A woman named Juanita answered the phone and asked me what I wanted to do. I told her I wanted to work in research because it would be a good starting ground for me. She replied, "The only job I have coming up is at *60 Minutes*."

I started off on the reception desk, a great place to begin—very collaborative. I met and became acquainted with everybody. Fortunately, I never felt in any way that I couldn't move up the ladder because I was a woman. It was tougher...don't get me wrong, but I never felt I couldn't do it. I used my talent and stuck it out. If you don't have perseverance and you get caught in that mire of "Oh, I can't do this, I'm a woman and they aren't going to give me a break," you won't make it. I think you have to pay attention to the prejudice women face, but keep moving forward.

All the women did research. They had a few women producers when I started at *60 Minutes* in 1981 but no female correspondents until Diane Sawyer arrived three years later.

Working at *60 Minutes* was a perfect fit for me—I felt very lucky to land in such a great place. One year after I started, Mike Wallace's assistant went on maternity leave and didn't know if she would return. The unit manager told me that Mike's assistant was *definitely* coming back and she strongly encouraged me not to take the job. If Mike's assistant wanted her job back, she wouldn't be able to give me another job. My instinct and perhaps my young age told me to take a chance, go for the opportunity. No matter how it turned out, it would be the experience of a lifetime. And it was...his assistant never came back!

People say Mike is a very difficult person to work with, but I never experienced that. I valued him in a different way. He and my father had similar personalities. They were the same age and their birthdays were two days apart. When I told people that he reminded me of my father, they would shake their heads. "Your father must have been tough!" Tough and difficult—yes on both counts for both men—but their intelligence and sense of fair play made up for it. Though my dad had a softer, sweeter side, he prepared me to understand Mike's point of view. They were similar in a good way for me. Being around Mike Wallace is what made me a better journalist.

As time went on, I went from Mike's assistant, to researcher, to associate producer and finally to producer. It was tough for a woman to become producer; a man could achieve the position easier. Men came in and were given a producing job right away without any experience. I know this because I helped one of them learn the ropes.

Ultimately, I worked with all of the *60 Minutes* correspondents: Morley Safer, Ed Bradley, Harry Reasoner, Meredith Vieira, Lesley Stahl, and Steve Kroft. I interviewed Bill and Hillary Clinton before they went to the White House, Gerald Ford after he left the White House, Wynton Marsalis, Kevin Spacey, Michael Caine and many others. I met Paul McCartney at a young age—wow! Traveling to and working in the Middle East for the first time changed the way I looked at the world. Here I was a kid from small-town America reporting on one of the biggest news stories of the century—the ongoing conflict between the Israelis and the Palestinians. How many journalists get to cover and report on that up close and personal? The answer is, not many, and I have to say that I feel very fortunate to have had the opportunity to not only meet and interview the men, women and children who were affected by the conflict on a daily basis, but I also got to interview some of the top spokespeople and decision-makers at the time—Hanan Ashrawi, Benjamin Netanyahu and Yasser Arafat.

Most of the people I've been privileged to meet and interview are not famous—their willingness to tell their stories has had a tremendous impact on me both personally and professionally. When I produced a piece on the Challenger space shuttle disaster, I interviewed one of the engineers who helped design and build the faulty rockets that caused the accident. He told me on the phone what happened the night before the launch and he burst into tears. It was very painful for him to tell that story again, but he did it. The camera crew said it was the best, most emotional *60 Minutes* story they had ever worked on. Hearing the story first hand from the people who were there, not just pundits who have read about it, makes *60 Minutes* the most successful news magazine in the history of television. I feel very fortunate to have been even a small part of that.

What other profession allows you to learn something new all the time and get to the truth? That is the heart of journalism to me, serving people by giving them the information they need to change the world. As a journalist, you are always trying to get information from people, being sympathetic to their story, and trying to show how their story affects others. I would like to think the work I did at *60 Minutes* touched people.

Before I left CBS, I saw a listing for a producer to work in Jordan. I had good credentials and had already worked in the Middle East, so they took an interest in me and offered me the opportunity. Leaving CBS after 30 years was not easy to do. But the timing was right because everything changes and moves forward. I had done some amazing work for CBS and *60 Minutes,* but life marches on. If I didn't do it at this point in my life, I would get too comfortable. I floated around *60 Minutes*, not advancing at any level with Mike Wallace's retirement and Ed Bradley's passing. The Jordan job offered a new landscape for me. I haven't regretted it, although I am certainly nervous about my future. I feel very positive because I did what I wanted to do at CBS.

My mother was a methodical woman and I inherited my determination and drive from her. My grandmother, a nurse, started the first nursing home in Queens, New York. At the time, she worked at Bellevue Hospital while raising four children. Her husband had just died and one of her children was dying of leukemia. By necessity, she started taking in tenants to support her family. At her lowest point, she considered welfare, but couldn't bring herself to do it. She had to persevere. She built up quite a business. At one point, she had four homes. She was amazing.

I have learned that things always work out. I've gone on interviews and been told we are not going to hire you but would like to work with you, so please stay in touch. I would call back and they would not answer. I would wonder what happened between this date and that date. But then I would realize something else happened that had nothing at all to do with me. It is good to remember there are many people in the same situation. Knowing you are not alone is a good thing. It keeps you level.

I did a training seminar in Jordan about a year after I left CBS. I realized that when I work, I do not worry about things I cannot change: "What have I done, what have I contributed, what will I do next?" I feel comfortable talking about my experience and accomplishments. Before, I would have considered it an ego thing, but I discovered that I could talk about my skills to teach and help others, and give back. I have experience they can learn from. That's where I am going now. I want to work on an international level because it's important for those who don't have a free press. We may not be happy with media here all the time, but it's free.

I have incredible respect for journalism. It's a tough road, but rewarding.

Human Resources

"I was thought to be a 'weak one on the council' because a woman was always the weak one...she could be intimidated and would tone down. Of course, it didn't work."

—*Nina Miglionico*
(1914–2009) Lawyer and former councilwoman,
Recipient of Margaret Brent Award

DELORES KESLER

Delores Kesler grew up on a chicken farm and never graduated from college. She also never allowed anyone to restrict her dreams or define them. She became the first woman to take a company public on Wall Street...and it was her own company. Accustaff, Incorporated, now Modis, Inc., was founded in 1978 with $10,000. Delores took it to the "Street" in 1994 and when she retired, it was generating $2 billion.

In 1998, she was the winner of the Horatio Alger Award and in 2002, she was honored with the Silver Medallion from NCCJ, National Conference for Community and Justice, for improving the quality of life in her hometown, Jacksonville, Florida. Florida Trend *named her one of the Most Influential Floridians and she was chosen by Dan Rather as one of eight people that epitomized the* American Dream *in his book of the same name.*

She has served as Director for the St. Joe Company, PSS/World Medical, Thermoview Industries and others. Always a believer in giving back to her community, she founded the Kesler Mentoring Connection as a tool in assisting youth and created the Kesler Endowment at the University of North Florida.

Her accolades, awards and achievements are numerous, but it was her ability to "go beyond what fell in my lap" that made her unique.

The Way I See It...

Have your own goals and don't let anyone set limits on you, whether they love you or not.

A First for Wall Street

My career began in 1961 at International Harvester, now Navistar, a large national company that sold trucks. I worked full time in the personnel department and went to college at night. I was divorced and supporting my small child, widowed mother and younger brother. The college tuition was expensive but I had always believed in a good education. I heard about Harvester's college tuition refund program and applied for it. They turned me down. "This program is limited to males who would probably have a sales future with our company. We take no female applicants." Yes, they could do that back then.

I told my boss, Robert Walls, who was quite visionary and open about things. He said, "You know that really isn't fair?"

I said "No, it's not, but they told me very clearly that I had to be a man and they wanted people focused on a sales career." I told him I wanted a sales career.

"We don't have any women in sales, but I tell you what...you get another one of those applications and bring it to me and let's fill it in together. Let's not put Delores, let's just put your initials."

I put DM and no name. At that time, no mark for male or female appeared on the paperwork. They would assume I was a man. Mr. Walls signed it and sent it directly to Chicago instead of through the regional office in Atlanta. His signature meant that he was recommending me. They wouldn't ask who or what I was. He even put a little note on the back and it came back approved!

Mr. Walls sat me down in his office to talk. "Now listen, you are the first woman to go to college and have this company pay for it. Sooner or later, they're going to figure it out. You better do well and have a good grade point average."

Three years later, the company sent their vice president of educational programs to Jacksonville for a meeting with employees enrolled in the tuition program. Around 100 people were involved and my name was on the list. When I walked into the meeting, the vice president standing at the front of the room noticed me. "Honey, you must be in the wrong room 'cause this meeting is for the men who are on the college tuition program."

With nervous pride, I said, "I am on that program."

"No, no, now darlin', your name has to be on this list." I pointed to my name and he looked surprised. "That's you?"

"That's me."

He was obviously flabbergasted. "How long have you been on this program?"

I told him three years.

He could only manage to say two words. "Sit down."

My boss was so proud. "This should have been done a long time ago. Yes, we were a little devious, but it's fair devious. You're not lying—you're not saying you're a man. You did it fair and square." He was my first mentor and his advice made a difference in my life. "Don't take no for an answer. Don't let them tell you that you can't do it." I was 21 years old and I was ready to say okay and fold. He wouldn't let me. "Don't do that. If you think you ever want to be in sales, you can't take no for an answer."

That experience taught me that a door may not always open for me. At times, I would have to create my own door or climb over a wall or go around, but there is a way. For the first time, I realized I had to make my own way in the world, including my desire to be in my own business.

When I started my career, women worked in a suppressive atmosphere with a glass ceiling clearly visible. They couldn't go into sales; the most a woman could expect was a department manager somewhere. In my mind, women were the workhorses who did all of the work. The men made the decisions and took all the glory. Many smart female workhorses knew they would never go beyond their positions. Even if I could do the job better than my boss, I knew that no opportunity to advance existed. It's what fueled that already latent desire to be an entrepreneur.

I found myself constantly meddling in authority. I knew I needed my own business to do what I wanted to do. While setting up programs or truck and tractor shows, I often shared ideas with Mr. Walls and he listened to them. He told me that I should own a business. I became excited about the staffing business—setting up truck shows in Atlanta, calling ahead to Kelly Girl or Manpower to hire temporary people—other women to act as secretaries or receptionists. I thought, "Isn't this neat? You pick up the phone and when you get to Atlanta, you have 20 people waiting on you!" I calculated that using human capital and being able to access it, evaluate it and work with it came natural to me.

Most people start their entrepreneurial venture a little earlier than I did. I was 37. The year was 1978. I was married with two children and no capital. I put together a business plan that included borrowing $50,000. The banks didn't want to lend money to a woman. My husband, who had a printing business that I helped him establish, had no money to spare and wouldn't sign for me to take out a loan on the house. "This is not the right time. You have two children and a good career and you're making good money. We need your salary because I have an entrepreneurial business. Maybe we can talk about a new business 10 years from now when the kids are out of school and my business is going well…"

The banks and my husband had no confidence in me, but I didn't take no for an answer. I went to 10 more banks and they all turned me down. I had no co-signer and nothing to use for equity.

I wasn't about to give up. I knew the president of a branch bank in Orange Park. We had been in the National Honor Society in high school. He stated the facts honestly. "Delores, I know you are blessed with fairly good brain power…but I don't see anything here that would allow me to loan you $50,000. I would never get this past the loan committee."

I still refused to accept defeat. "How much can you loan me without having to go to your loan committee?"

"All I can do is $10,000."

I could see a way around the door. "Loan it to me and I will pay you back."

"How can you do that?"

"I'll use my expertise—I'm gonna do it all myself."

I could see how nervous he was as he walked me to the door of the bank. "Delores, I can't afford to take a $10,000 hit on this. Don't you dare let me down."

In six months, I paid back the $10,000 and the bank loaned me the $50,000. It was just something that was absolutely meant to be. I shouldn't have been able to start a business on $10,000…one that ultimately became a $2 billion public company when I retired in 1997. I never had a partner, no venture capital. I put the money in it and owned 100% of it and built it to a $50 million company before we went public.

When I took my company public, I was the only woman that owned a major staffing company. I wanted to grow my company from $50 million to $1 billion. I couldn't do it privately, so I started talking to my staffing buddies around the country. Only a few major staffing companies existed at that time—basically Manpower, Adia, and Kelly. We needed to take four or five regional staffing companies to form one and take it public. They all laughed at me. It took me a year to find three male partners from across the country. We combined our companies with about $100 million in revenue and went public in 1994.

My company had the largest in revenue with the other two totaling $50 million. Since I had built my company from the ground up, I had earned the respect of the other owners. The investment bankers were another story.

When I told the investors that I was going to take the company public, they told me I couldn't do it. "There's never been a woman chairman or CEO who has taken a company public. Wall Street is not going to buy it. You are not going to be credible."

I had to recruit a man from Coopers Lybrand CPA and bring him in as CFO, and then president. When we went public, I promoted myself to executive chairman and made him CEO. The company hired another male as CFO. I surrounded myself with financial acumen so investors couldn't question my credentials. "This woman didn't even graduate college, how is she going to do this?" We went public with a little over $100 million. After a few acquisitions, we were in a run rate of $2 billion when I retired.

A real male bias exists on Wall Street. A big part of the male world applauded when Carly Fiorina, former CEO of Hewlett-Packard, went down. The men saw her fall as justification. "See, a woman shouldn't have been doing that in the first place." That sentiment has not gone away. I have heard men discuss situations where women failed. "Oh, a woman...she was over her head anyway." If a man had gotten into that same situation, they wouldn't have said, "It's because he's a man." They would have said that he had a bad set of circumstances. So the bias still exists and we can't hide it and stick our heads in the sand and say it is an absolute level playing field. It is not. But the field is not so tilted that a woman can't get around it with creativity and change it for the better. I could always go beyond what fell into my lap.

I have been totally blessed with opportunities to experience more than I ever dreamed. I had my own goals and didn't let anyone set limits for me, whether they loved me or not. If you talked to people who worked with me when I made cutting edge decisions, they would say that I pioneered the way for women. I took time to mentor and counsel at my company. I never allowed people to say they couldn't do something because they were a woman. I insisted on gender and racial diversity. At a national CEO conference in 1985, we brought our assistants. I looked around the room and every other CEO was male and all their assistants were cute and Caucasian. My assistant was an attractive African-American. When we entered the room, the others looked at us with jaws dropping. I didn't do it for shock because it should not have been shocking to anybody, anyway.

I have been willing to step out on the ledge. Women might say, "She did those things so that I can." I am by nature a risk taker if I believe in what I am doing. My business partners call me Pollyanna with my positive attitude, but I have never worried about what other people have said about me.

You need to believe in something. Have a cause you feel strongly about. Most contributing and successful people have a cause. It doesn't have to be business related, just something outside of yourself. You can't just go to work and go home and do nothing...you have to give back.

Things haven't been easy for me, but they have been doable. I have been willing to pay the price to do them by taking advantage of situations that some people were not willing to do. There is a price to pay. There's no free lunch. When you have a spouse, children and career, something gets the short shrift. I've never seen an entrepreneur that didn't work 60 to 70 hours a week. It's a real balancing act.

Marketing

NANN MILLER

Nann Miller was the first woman to attend the Rotary Club in Los Angeles, where her greatest asset was being a woman. She began her career in Chicago for the Playboy Club, although not as a Bunny. As a TV producer, she produced the forerunner of Saturday Night Live. *She also worked directly with Sargent and Eunice Kennedy Shriver on the first Special Olympics.*

Upon moving to Los Angeles, she started Miller/Geer & Associates Public Relations. After a long and prosperous career, she sold her company to a former student from her days on the Cal State and UCLA extension faculties.

The Los Angeles Times *dubbed her the "Queen of Special Events" and she is one of the original recipients of the title "Fellow" and the Accredited in Public Relations credential by the Public Relations Society of America. She has won over 45 awards.*

Her projects garnered five mentions in the Guinness Book of World Records: *the World's Largest Root Beer Float for Proctor and Gamble; the World's Longest Fashion Show; the World's Largest Sundae for Walt Disney; and the World's Largest Photograph for the City of Los Angeles.*

Her meaningful work with organizations such as the Airline Pilots Association and the Society for the Prevention of Cruelty to Animals changed laws; and events such as the Golden Gate Bridge 50th Anniversary and the Statue of Liberty 200th Birthday Celebration allowed many people to reap the benefits.

She says not a day goes by that something she has worked on... some program that she began...is not on TV as someone else's work.

The Way I See It...

Women tend to get too hung up on sex in the workplace. My advice is to give the man a hug, say you are glad he has good taste, tell him it sounds like fun but isn't on your schedule for the week, and walk away.

No Crocodile Tears

I never saw a glass ceiling. I assumed if I was going to succeed in the male world, it was not because of legislation or fairness to my gender. My success was a result of making those who paid me successful. I also assumed that obstacles were part of the rise up the ladder. The 1970s were the best time in history for women to break into business. The competition was less fierce. Men wanted to throw us a bone that led to much more. Impossible situations made my success. Most women had already given up or were afraid to try, so there weren't that many of us. We stood out...all alone...*with all the opportunities.*

At my Public Relations Society of America, PRSA, events, I was a special person. The men treated me like royalty. It used to be 93% men and 7% women. Today, it's the opposite, the extreme opposite, and not as much fun. The glass ceiling is gone. It's sad. I would be on the same level as a man if I were 22 years old again and working.

Maybe I like men too much. I love flirting, love all the wonderful feelings and experiences...especially the feedback I get from men. Being attractive was a plus for me and I don't know if it would be that much of a plus anymore. I'm glad that I started working when I did.

I worked the conventions as a hostess or narrator in the McCormick Center in Chicago for my first jobs. Talk about sexist...all the men would whistle and stare at me! I wore short shorts and had long legs and I truly had a great figure. I worked the auto shows and many of the men would whisper in my ear, "Say, honey, I'll give you in 10 minutes what you're making all day." I had a job with a Kohler plumbing product...*in a shower*. I wasn't nude, but the men would proposition me as if I was a prostitute. They were from somewhere like Kansas City, most likely alone, away from home. I didn't reflect on their comments as insulting to me...it was a reflection of their loneliness. They would hand me their room keys from the Palmer House and I would just smile. I thought, "If I was fat and grisly looking, they wouldn't be doing this."

I lived in two worlds—one, the suburban world with my kids in grade school and me, the little housewife at home; and the other world where I worked as the model, hostess or interviewer. I never told people what I did...even my friends didn't know. Sometimes they saw me catching a train to go into the city. Once, a modeling agency wanted a sexy looking girl to interview people about their travel habits at O'Hare Airport. I gladly took the job and enjoyed it until I saw my neighbors headed in my direction. I ran. My children played with their children, and I thought my neighbors might be uptight about the situation. I didn't want my job to hurt my children in any way.

If people found out that I was working for the agency, I would hear comments. "She'll be sorry when her kids grow up to be inmates. I hope she knows what she's doing." Pretty wrong observations as my children are all super successful today...all five of them! According to the social norm of the day, I was supposed to stay home and raise my children. I gave my two days a week to the PTA and found a good babysitter. I served as a den mother for the cub scouts and worked in the school cafeteria. I was friends with all the neighbors, but I just didn't mix my two lives. I didn't brag about it and I didn't do it for the money. I had a need not to be bored.

Alice Baker, a top model, lived on my street. We became close friends. We both knew that our lives wouldn't mix well with our neighbors, so we didn't try. I don't remember worrying about it. They would have been annoyed more than anything else, so what would have been the point in annoying women who chose to live life differently from me? I wasn't trying to prove anything to them.

I only remember being discriminated against once. I auditioned to be a television news commentator in Chicago at WMAQ. I was a co-producer of several shows at the time, but I wanted to be a "Katie Couric." I was definitely rejected because I was a woman. No women led the news in 1968, only Walter Cronkite. I certainly had more abilities than some of the men. They blamed my accent, but that was an excuse. I didn't mope about it and march down State Street and protest. I decided that's just the way it is. I'll go around life another way.

I was one of the first women in Chicago in public relations. I landed a job with a third rated property called the LaSalle Hotel and my soon to be profitable agency was born. But as life would have it, my husband had to move to Los Angeles and I just knew I couldn't begin a public relations agency there.

Luckily when we arrived in California, the management gurus believed public relations would benefit from a woman's touch. They saw women as "good-will ambassadors." As a result, I became the first public relations executive for the California Mart. I stayed five years and learned the business before starting Nann Miller Enterprises, my own company.

My first client, Hyatt Hotels, stayed with me 17 years. My company is still one of LA's most prestigious companies, known as Miller Geer Arizmendez.

I can't remember a boss who didn't ask me to bed when I started out. It was always a joke, and yes, I could have risen to the bait. One man in particular always arose from his desk to open the door for me when our meeting ended. As I walked out, he would touch my breast…totally unacceptable behavior. He would make some kind of joke out of it. It was his problem, not mine. I did not want to lose the wonderful opportunity to work on his project; however, I had to weigh this in my mind. He owned eight hotels and provided me with enormous amounts of experience. I wasn't getting in bed with him…it was just that thing that he did. I let it be. Some may think I was wrong, but it certainly hasn't changed my life in any way.

Women tend to get too hung up on sex in the workplace. My advice is to give the man a hug, say you are glad he has good taste, tell him it sounds like fun but isn't on your schedule for the week, and walk away. I never put anybody down. I guess I don't have the same way of looking at things as other women.

I was constantly in and out of hotels, traveling and eating by myself. It was lonely. I felt empathy for lonely people who had bitchy wives back home. I had the chance to say yes or no, and one time, somebody did knock on my door. I didn't get all huffy and puffy—I never had that attitude. I could always call the front desk, but I never had to. I just ignored it.

In the eighties, the Hyatt Los Angeles was my client, and I had lunch there almost every day. The Rotary Club met there too. The law had recently passed requiring Rotary Clubs to admit women. They needed a woman, so they asked me to join. I pondered the invitation. "Why would I want to be in the Rotary?" The manager at the Hyatt told me it would be good for business—the Rotary was a profitable account for the hotel. I joined. A wealthy society woman who owned a bank was a member, but since she never came to meetings, I was officially the first woman to attend.

After a presidential election, the Rotary Club president asked everyone at the meeting who voted Republican to stand up. Everybody in the room stood up except for a black man and me. A white man sitting next to me said, "You realize if your candidate had won, we would all have lost our privileges?"

I said, "I'm trying to figure out what you are telling me...that because I am a Democrat and a woman, you could lose your privileges?"

He said, "You got it, sister."

Did I care? No. It was his problem.

"Well, being divorced is like being hit by a Mack truck. If you live through it,
you start looking very carefully to the right and to the left."

—Jean Kerr
(1922–2003) American playwright & humorist

MARGARET CUSTER FORD

Margo Ford worked for Welcome Wagon before launching her business, MARCO Ideas Unlimited, a promotional products company in 1959. One of five women and the only person from the Pacific Northwest, she was named one of the 50 most influential people in the past 50 years in her profession. She received the honor, "National Person of the Year" formerly known as "National Man of the Year" by the Advertising Specialty Institute in Philadelphia. Her greatest honor was her induction into the National Hall of Fame by Promotional Products Association International, an organization of several thousand members with one vote per firm. Only three women have ever achieved that goal.

The Way I See It...

An advantage of being a woman in business is that we listen between the lines to reach a desired solution.

Pioneer in Oregon

When my five year marriage ended in divorce, I had two little girls and $125 per month in child support. It was time to do something more lucrative. I worked as a Welcome Wagon hostess and had a terrible time finding anyone who could suggest suitable products and where to buy them. I discovered a national company, Brown and Bigelow, as a source for gift ideas. Here my journey began in the promotional products industry.

I was turned down for the interview with the district manager in Portland when I applied for a sales job at Brown and Bigelow: "Women just don't work out...we hire men." I tried to convince him to give me a chance, but he wouldn't even meet with me. I told him I knew of several women who worked as sales reps for his company in other parts of the country. "Oh well," he said, "those are just widows of men who formerly worked for us. We allow them to take the orders that would have been placed with their husbands. Women just don't work out well for us."

"Nuts," I thought. "I'll just do it myself and show you that women can do just fine in this business." I was 30 years old when I started my company. Years later, I had several employees from Brown and Bigelow apply for work with my company. It seemed they had filed bankruptcy. That man actually did me a favor. His rejection made me all the more competitive.

Society expected women in the 1950s to be stay-at-home moms. If that was not possible, they might be teachers, secretaries, nurses or sales clerks. My friends and family worried about me. "Why don't you just go be a secretary somewhere so you can be sure of an income? What if it doesn't work out?"

I pushed on, but it was tough. Manufacturers and suppliers didn't want to deal with women. I used my initials M.C. to write letters because my sex couldn't be identified. When I requested suppliers, I heard the same thing over and over. "We are sufficiently covered in your geographical area." I even sent a road map to the manufacturers outlining that Medford, Oregon was 300 miles south of Portland and 400 plus miles north of San Francisco. No distributors existed in between those two cities.

Of course, my brand new, fledgling business with no credit history certainly had a bearing on the situation. Credit cards didn't exist, but a few companies let me place business orders with a pre-payment or partial payment for the orders. I couldn't even say that I was experienced in the field and had previously worked for a known industry company, because I hadn't. The only way I could present products to potential clients was with catalogs or samples.

One day, I received a call from Bob Yaw of Cedar Rapids, Iowa. He was the CEO of one of the oldest and largest pen and pencil manufacturing companies in the business. He apologized for his credit department.

They had erred in telling several firms that they didn't know who I was when the firms called for my references. He wrote personal letters to the heads of the supplier firms that had denied me and recommended they give me a chance. I couldn't believe it.

I stood out and the other companies took notice because I was a woman. The heads of large companies didn't compare notes about a new company on the west coast unless there was a reason. I could almost imagine the conversation. "Say, Bob, did you know there is a woman who is starting a distributorship out in Oregon? Can you imagine, a woman?"

When I went to my first national trade show, only two women walked the floors as buying principals in their own firms. I heard later that out of the 3,000 or so member firms in the national association, only two were women. I remember Ann Morrissey, another woman in the industry, discussing the circumstance of women in business. "We must do the job right. The women coming behind us will benefit from our efforts to be as good as we can be. We must be better than the men or they will say, 'We knew you couldn't do it. Why don't you just go home and crochet?'"

Being called on by a female was a novelty to male buyers. Some were determined to test my mettle, so I learned it was important to smile and be firm. I acted in a lady-like, yet assertive manner. When the conversation drifted off track, I learned how to bring it back again and do it graciously. An occasional pass was made, but I learned how to fend it off. I've heard women complain about sexual harassment but it didn't happen with me. Maybe I wasn't good looking enough. If any kind of innuendo or suggestion was made, I usually smiled and said, "Oh, I don't think your wife would like that and I doubt my husband would either." Then, I would continue with my proposal. I laugh when I remember another special friend of mine's retort to any advances: "That is flattering, but no...one of us would be sure to be disappointed, and I wouldn't want it to be me!" That would cause the man to smile, recognize that she wasn't putting him down, but the answer was no.

In general, we operated in a more formal atmosphere in those days. Letters began with "Gentlemen" or "Dear Sir." Ladies wore hats, gloves, hose and never *ever* pantsuits. Throughout Oregon, Washington, and Northern California, I was careful not to be too dressed up when calling on manufacturing plants and lumber mills. I wore understated clothes when I called on men in hard hats and work clothes. I wore absolutely no jewelry. When I worked with banks and insurance companies, I could dress in a more sophisticated way, but never in pants.

An advantage of being a woman in business is that we listen better and we listen between the lines to reach a desired solution. Because we are softer and more caring, we are perceived as truly interested in creating solutions to a problem and not simply trying to gain our own ends.

However, being a female boss can be a challenge if an employee doesn't recognize your ability to lead. Both men and women employees can resent a woman's authority.

Since there were so few women business owners in those days, I was noticed. Visibility brought me chances for growth, increased leadership roles in organizations and appointments with potential clients who were curious as to what a woman might be able to do.

Financing was another issue completely. Meeting face to face, I couldn't hide my sex like I could in written correspondence. What a challenge! The banks wouldn't talk with me, even when I could prove that I had purchase orders well over the total of the requested loan amount. I had to have a friend co-sign a note for $500. Most men held the perception that women were "little ladies" incapable of making a business decision or paying for it once made. Women belonged at home in the kitchen.

Shortly after moving to Portland, experiencing some success in my business, I was ready to buy that Mercedes sports car I had always wanted. I had been in business for nearly 20 years, owed no personal debt other than my home, and was driving a one-year old, loan free automobile. When I stopped at the dealership, I knew exactly what I wanted and busied myself in the showroom, looking into the trunk and storage areas, sitting in the seats. Finally the laid back salesman came ambling out of his office where he had been on the phone for a long time. "Nice car, isn't it, little lady?" He obviously would have preferred to talk to a man. He would be able to close the sale with someone like himself.

With an indulgent smile and condescending attitude, the salesman acted like a woman couldn't possibly be able to afford one of his cars. I went to another dealer in another town and purchased my dream car...a brand new 1977 Mercedes 450 SL. I loved it then and I love it now with over 200,000 miles on it.

Two months later, the first salesman called this "little lady" to tell me he had a beautiful car that would look great in my driveway. By then, he had checked me out and realized I could buy a car. Oh, what a pleasure I had in sweetly asking, "Do you think it would look any nicer than the one that is already there?"

Before I left Southern Oregon, I was immensely proud that I was able to develop a very large line of credit on my own personal signature at my bank. I was often told I was a pioneer. It made me feel as though I had come across the mountains in a covered wagon. Few women did what I did. I gave speeches and seminars knowing that what I said had to make sense and be "right" or other women wouldn't be given a chance. I was active in all the right clubs, took every possible educational opportunity to advance my career, hired women for my company and generally worked to be as good as I possibly could be.

When I was elected to the National Board of the Promotional Products Association the first time, I strived to prove that a woman can have a brain and still be friendly and courteous while sticking up for her principles. It made a difference to other women and made it easier for them to achieve.

My daughter once told me that she knew she could do anything she set her mind to do …because I had told her so, and made her believe it.

Transportation

JUNE M. MORRIS

June Morris was in the travel business for more than 30 years, earning distinction as the 33rd largest business owned and operated by a woman in the United States. She founded a travel agency in 1970, growing it into one of the largest in the nation. From it, she launched Morris Air Service, a full service airline to 28 cities, operating a fleet of 737 aircraft. One of her key people at Morris Air went on to start Jet Blue, another low-fare airline. She is most proud of being the company that brought low air fares to Utah.

In 1994 she won the Ernst & Young Entrepreneur of the Year Award, the same year she sold her company to Southwest Airlines. She then joined Southwest's Board of Directors and served for the next 12 years. She is one of only two women in the Utah Business Hall of Fame, and received tremendous publicity for being the first woman CEO of a major airline. She has served on many boards, including the Utah Governor's Commission on the Status of Women, the Board of Trustees for the Salt Lake Winter Games Organizing Committee and the Federal Reserve Board.

The Way I See It...

I have qualities men don't have. Why fight it? Go with it. Put that energy to work for you.

Low Air Fare Lady

I grew up in the 1930s with a working mother, a true role model. She was the first person to drive a car in her town and the other ladies thought she was wild. She played piano with a little bandstand considered really "naughty" in her day. She was also a businesswoman, serving as the first president of a ladies realtor group in Utah.

My dad had been raised in a wealthy family but they lost everything in the Depression. His father had raised stock, sheep and cattle. My dad eventually took over and when the banks failed, he lost so much that he was never quite the same. It took the wind out of his sails. He was a great guy and everybody loved him, but my mother was the driving force in our family. She had to be after the Depression hit. Fortunately, she loved the real estate business. She exuded excitement when she made a sale. She was a go-getter.

The reason I went into business was because of my husband's encouragement. I had been working at a travel agency and he didn't like my rigid schedule. To suit him, I quit and came home. I lasted about six months before boredom overtook me. I told him I wanted to get a job again. He said, "Oh no, you don't. Why don't you start your own business?" He was a successful business person, an owner of a chain of photo finishing plants that he eventually sold to Transamerica. He believed in me and I did it.

I ordered brochures for my one woman travel agency. Several airline people dismissed me. "You shouldn't be going into this business to get free trips. You're being foolish." I made them rethink their position when I landed every big account in the state...it was fun! My little travel agency eventually became the biggest one in Utah, beyond my wildest imagination. I bounced a little airline off of it with about 23 airplanes. Not a huge endeavor as far as airlines, but I had a real going concern.

It never occurred to me that being a woman was a problem. I used it to my advantage. Various company account representatives would often ask, "Do you think we should speak with your husband about that?"

My response was always, "Sure…but he doesn't know what's going on." I got a big kick out of that.

People never offended me. They would ask if I were so and so's secretary. I would say, "Sure." It was never an issue with me. I absolutely used this to my advantage. I think women who don't use these misconceptions to their own benefit are missing a big opportunity.

Women can appeal to people on a different basis than men. No doubt about it. I never take no for an answer, but I can do it in a way that a man cannot possibly do. I can gracefully beg to get what I want; whereas, it just wouldn't work for a man. One of my biggest customers with the travel agency was Sperry Univac. The head of the company wanted a big suite in a hotel at a very busy time. I called the hotel and begged sweetly, "You've got to help me…I really need this." Can you imagine a man doing that? It wouldn't work. When I was working with American Express Travel, if anybody needed anything they couldn't get, I could get it. I was able to convince people that I needed their help.

This ability helps when you have men working for you. Some men can't take direction from other men without feeling their egos stepped on. Yet I could appeal to them in a motherly way. I could finesse a situation and get away with it—tell them things they didn't want to hear without them getting mad at me.

In a serious crisis with a customer who was trying to make us pay $500,000 for something that wasn't our fault, I started crying. I did it on purpose. I believe the man went to his home office and told them to "get this woman off my back!" It wasn't that I was faking it…it was just my personality. I let myself be female instead of acting like I was a tough businessman. I allowed myself to go with my emotions. I wasn't being sneaky about it…I was just doing what came natural to me as a female.

I was thrilled to be a woman-owned business. Everybody knew it…it was in my name. I started it and developed it. My status was a benefit because the government was required to do business with women and minorities to meet quotas. Numbers for travel were large because airline tickets were much higher then and they could take care of their whole quota by doing business with me. It was part of my pitch. If someone was competing against me, all things equal, I got the contracts.

I put the female touch on our company…different than a man would have done. It grew like a family. A large board posted photos of employees' grandkids as if they were my grandkids. Parties had a family atmosphere. An interesting culture developed, almost identical to Southwest Airlines. We called ours *Morris Magic* and they called theirs *Southwest Spirit*. Industry insiders said that the world's best airline merger was Morris Air and Southwest Airlines because the cultures were absolutely similar. Current Southwest Airlines President Colleen Barrett has kept that kind of family and caring atmosphere going. That is what I did from day one. Today, Colleen and I are very good friends...we have always had much in common.

It was a natural instinct as a woman to build a friendly and helpful atmosphere. The female nurturing qualities help build a strong culture. I know some feminists would think this is a bunch of bull. I am telling it like it was for me. Certain feminists are always complaining about how they are treated. I don't understand that because I have never felt mistreated. But I have a feeling that some of them are trying to prove they are tough and strong and as good as a man. Competing with men was not important to me. I have qualities men don't have. Why fight it? Go with it. Put that energy to work for you.

As our culture changed, women began to receive recognition for their contributions. I saw the status of women steadily improve. I agree problems still exist in the workforce for women trying to move up in a company, especially through the rank and files. In a corporate culture, you have to be better than men to get the advancements and salaries. It's harder for women to get to the top, and they have to be outstanding to get there and stay.

One way women can escape this double standard is to head up their own company. My company was not huge. We had a couple of thousand employees when we sold to Southwest. Size wasn't our most important accomplishment. Our best contribution was bringing low fares to Utah 12 years sooner than when Southwest came into the market. It made a huge difference in Utah. Many businesses opened up and people were able to conduct business outside of the state due to our low fares. That was the reason I was inducted into the Utah Business Hall of Fame—and I am honored.

I was concerned about being a role model for women, hoping I gave out the right message. In my office, I was "Lucy Brown...the doctor is in...5 cents please." I heard everybody's stories. I enjoyed that. And it helped people. I have encouraged young women to become successful in business. I was very visible in the public eye, in the news all the time. *Business Week* and *USA Today* ran articles about me as the first woman CEO of an airline. I don't believe there has been another one.

I would have hated being a man if I had to do it all over again. I can tell you it would not have been any easier.

And no, I never learned to fly...I took some lessons but I was a chicken. It was really scary. When I flew in our simulators, I crashed. On the other hand, I built my company from the ground up, flying higher than I had ever dreamed possible.

Actress

"The young men of today who have been fortunate enough to have a strong female parent seem to have a new perspective on women and our incredible worth."

—Dee Cook
Retired Educator, Huntington, West Virginia

ANGELINA C. TORRES

Angie Torres was raised by her Spanish immigrant parents on a farm in Albuquerque, New Mexico. Her story is like Cinderella's—as a child, she worked like a dog every day; then, at the age of 19, she married an older man and remained married for 35 years. Finally, surprising even herself, she became a Hollywood actress at age 60. She has appeared in 35 movies, including The Missing *with Tommy Lee Jones and Cate Blanchett;* Fools Rush In *with Matthew Perry and Salma Hayek;* Streets of Laredo *with James Garner, Sissy Spacek and Sam Shepard; and* Mad Love *with Chris O'Donnell and Drew Barrymore.*

Among her many accolades are the Governor's Award for Outstanding Women and the New Mexico Distinguished Public Service Award.

Author's Note: Ms. Torres passed away after her interview and before the publication of this book.

The Way I See It...

Now that I am older and more experienced, I realize I could have talked back. I didn't think my life was difficult at the time; it was expected.

Putting on an Act

When my dad died, it was the best thing that ever happened to my family. It was God's blessing. He had miner's lung disease because he was a hard headed old miner who would work two shifts and refuse to wear a mask. He ended up choking to death on his own blood in the hospital. That was the happiest day of my life.

He was a very cruel, vicious man who only knew hard work. Because I was a woman and could not work like a man in the coal mines, he beat me all the time. It was just crazy. To this day, I remember standing beside him and urinating all over myself...waiting to just get out of his way. He was brutal. In his mind, women were only good for two things, to keep your bed warm and give you sons, not daughters. I solemnly took my mother's advice. "Keep your mouth shut and stay out of your father's way. If you see him coming, move."

After my mother gave birth to one of my brothers, my father walked into the room and saw her cradling her newborn in the bed. "What in the name of heaven are you doing in bed at this time of day? Get up from there and have me something on the table to eat. I'm hungry and I've been working." When she told him she had just given birth, he leaned in closer to her. "I don't care if you've got 10 new babies...get out of that bed and fix me something to eat!" And she did. She fixed him something to eat.

When he died, I thought my mother could have a little freedom, but instead the worst thing happened: *she* died. My mother was my best friend. She gave me the only affection I had ever known. She taught me everything...how to bake bread, wash with a washboard, iron, darn socks, can food and all the other chores on the farm. She bled to death, always in poor health because of her hard life.

In 1934, I was forced to quit school and become the mother at 14 years of age. It's what I was trained to do. My brothers were grown men and wanted home-made bread and a pot of garbanzo beans on the table and their white shirts ironed. Taking care of the family became my full time job.

I was allowed to date only occasionally and my brothers made it clear to me. "You come back pregnant, by God, and we'll kill you."

I had my orders. "Make sure my white shirt is clean because I'm going out tonight…I'm bringing some people home to eat and you'd better have enough on the table."

That was my life. I was completely surrounded and dominated by males. I never knew I could talk back. I was afraid they would kick me in the face. My mother had protected me all the time and after she died, I was scared all the time. Now that I am older and more experienced, I realize I could have talked back. I didn't think my life was difficult at the time; it was expected. They told me exactly what to do. I had no say-so. It is not a pretty story, but it is true.

I finally went back to high school. I was even offered a scholarship to go to college but, of course, I couldn't take it. I still had the responsibility of my younger brother and sister.

At age 19, I married a man from Spain, 11 years older than me. He wanted a large family and I gave him one…five children, all still living. Of course, his idea of a woman was the same as my father and brothers: she was to belong to the man and do what he asked. A wife was not to think, read or write poetry. She was strictly his possession. He loved me dearly, don't get me wrong, but he only knew one way—the selfish male imposed way of domination. Since I had never been allowed to dominate, I didn't miss it. We were married 35 years.

I was 54 years old when he died of stroke, high blood pressure.

I asked my good friend, "What am I going to do with my life now? I don't know how to do anything but take care of a husband and children. I will just sit back and do nothing."

She said, "Young lady, that is not good enough. We'll find something for you to do."

I started volunteering at the YWCA.

In high school, I had tried out for a play, along with my little brother. We won a prize for our acting two years in a row. My friend knew about this honor and pointed me in that direction. "We'll get you a job in the theatre."

I said, "I can't do that. My husband would kill me."

I'll never forget the look she gave me. "Your husband is dead and so will you be in another year if you don't straighten out. Now get over there and do this."

I auditioned and they liked me. I couldn't giggle on cue, but they still liked me! I eventually learned to giggle. I did 60 plays and enjoyed it. With time, they started to become more difficult. My friend decided I should act in a movie. Again, I said, "I can't do that."

Naturally, she ignored me. "Come on, you can read for a part."

And I was cast in a Hallmark movie of the week, *Stones for Ibarra*, with Glenn Close and Keith Carradine. I told my friend, "I have no more business doing this than flying to the moon. This is terrible. What if I fall flat on my face?"

Glenn Close was a wonderful woman and she took me under her wing. She was pregnant at the time and even shared with me the name of the father, but wouldn't tell anyone else. She was so thoughtful and knew I was scared to death. She brought me a wrapped gift and said, "This is to celebrate your first day on the set, because I know how hard it was for me on the first day." That was one of the nicest things…especially since she was so ill with morning sickness. She was delightful to take the time to do that.

I have done 30 to 40 movies, mostly bit parts and sometimes plays. I play character roles well. They want a real old lady? Okay, I can play that. I'm not bragging; I am a very good actress. I can really put on an act. Plus, I am paid very well. *Fools Rush In* with Salma Hayek was my favorite movie and I still get residuals from it. Not that I need it, but it's always good to have spare change around.

My life is like Cinderella's, but my reward and escape has been theatre. I love it. If you are an aspiring actor and you like what you are doing, do it right. Listen, watch, and pick up on what's happening. Pay attention to the big, important actors: they don't act snotty and they take direction well. Don't be too big for your britches. Take it step by step and behave yourself on the set. When a good opportunity arises, you will be ready.

Politics

Patsy Riley

Coming from an idyllic movie-set childhood...playing hide and seek and catching lightning bugs until dark...Patsy Riley never dreamed she would one day become Alabama's First Lady.

For 20 years as a homemaker, she "invested in the future" and raised her four children. She suffered through the loss of her daughter, Jenice, but now, she is "investing in Alabama's future" by giving back to her state every day.

The Way I See It...

When the going gets tough, many people throw up their hands and say, "I am not going through that." We all need enough of that southern toughness, that steel magnolia down in your heart that says, "I care less what anyone else thinks. God has given me this plan and I am moving forward."

A Heart of Southern Steel

I had a charming childhood in small-town U.S.A. In the summer, we rode bikes and skated around the courthouse square. On hot days, we walked to the city pool and then later we waded in the creek. I can still feel how good it felt to slip into crisp sheets, fresh off the clothes line, after a hot bath to get rid of all the red bugs from playing outside.

Daddy was the town druggist and he came home every day for lunch, or dinner as we called it then. Daddy would never turn anyone away with a sick child. Many a Sunday dinner was interrupted by a knock on our wooden front door. When he opened the door, he would listen quietly to the problem before he ran for his jacket. "I'll be right up, you just wait out by the store across from the courthouse." Mama would fuss that we never got to eat Sunday dinner together, but Daddy always would say, "It could be one of our children sick and in pain. I'll be right back."

We saw people sitting out on porches and everyone knew everyone in town. Life was safe and quiet.

I got here from there by God's plan for my life and my husband, Bob Riley, the present Alabama governor. We went back to our hometown in 1965 after we married Christmas of '64. We thought we'd live there, raise our family there, grow old there and die there. But in 1994, after many successful businesses, Bob decided to run for U.S. Congress. After six years in Washington, he decided to run for Governor. When he won, I became First Lady. What a life! I went from being a stay-at-home mom and housekeeper to First Lady of the great state of Alabama.

I had thought my purpose in life was to be a good wife and mother to four children, educate them well, send them on their way, give them all the words of the Rock, give them the tools to minister to others and have a lot of joy in giving to others. I wanted them to also understand you can give yourself away and then there isn't anything else to give. I wanted to teach them to find balance.

As First Lady of Alabama, a whole new world of purpose opened up to me. My children were all raised at that point...all married but one. I became involved with charities helping in any way that I could while promoting Alabama as a spokesperson and ambassador. I never dreamed anyone would ask my opinion on my great state of Alabama. All of a sudden, I was given the opportunity to shine for Alabama and let Alabama shine through me. I have done work with organizations that support women and children. We have a task force working on a project for abused children because there are too many laws in place that protect the adult abuser. We are trying to change the laws so that a child does not go back to the abusive home and has a place of safety. A three-year old can't verbalize what has happened, and since there is no way to prove the abuser's guilt, the child goes right back into the same situation.

Another project we are working on is called PALS. WalMart has come on board as a partner and will put up signs and banners with a 1-800 number for people to call when their stress level reaches the point that they may abuse their family members. We will have billboard, radio and television ads that say, "If you are not an abuser, but you feel your stress level taking you to that place, please call this number for help." Hopefully, we can prevent abuse before it happens. They say that sometimes physical wounds will heal, but emotional wounds may never heal. I don't believe I would have ever gotten over being slapped around or being told I was no good as a child.

Growing up, I knew how far I could go. My mother would send me out to cut a "switch" so she could strike my little legs good and proper, but I never had to worry that either one of my parents would strike me and knock me onto the floor.

My life has been filled with purpose and success, but I have also faced times of anguish. The lowest point of my life was the loss of my daughter, Jenice. Elizabeth Jenice was 33 years old. She was diagnosed with cervical cancer, then ovarian cancer. The doctors warned us that so much chemotherapy would weaken her little organs by putting a lot of poison in her body. She never weighed more than 94 pounds, ever. She went through massive radiation, too, and that weakens all your blood vessels. She survived three years, and then, at about three o'clock one afternoon, she had a massive hemorrhage and passed over at 2:58 in the morning. It was very peaceful. She didn't fight it. We didn't fight it. She simply went to sleep and didn't wake up.

I wish I could say it made my faith stronger, but it didn't. I already had an unbelievable faith and strength. I truly believed and fully trusted and put it on the throne of grace. As the Bible says, "You have not because you ask not" and "Where two or more are gathered in my name, it will be." But it did *teach* me. I have grown stronger every day understanding it. God was feeding me the information I needed at the time and today I understand that God has an infinite plan.

Long before Jenice was born, or you and I were born, God knew what day and minute we were going to be born and what day and minute we were going to die and be taken back to Him. We are loaned out to be with our parents or children or husbands or families. We don't own them and they don't own us. I belong to God and the minute it is time for me to go, it will not matter who is praying for me, even if it is the Pope himself. When that time comes, my date Jesus will arrive at the door. He is not going to be a minute early or a minute late. He is going to meet me at the door.

I had to go through the experience with my child to know that all the prayers in the world weren't going to change it. All the doctors in the world weren't going to change it. My faith wasn't going to change it. Never one time did I believe she was not going to make it and not only make it, but have her miracle ministry. My faith was stronger at that point more than ever, but when it didn't happen, I promise you, it shook my world. When I had to stop and start reading and thinking to keep from losing my mind, that is when I realized, "Patsy, Thy will be done...not *my* will be done." I couldn't change it. That is how a parent keeps from going off the deep end. It takes all the responsibility off you and all the guilt off of you. "What if we had known sooner...what if we had gone to a different doctor...what if I had done something different when she was growing up...her female organs could have been stronger." You don't have to go back over every decision that was made medically or emotionally or physically. You can make something of your life instead of continuing to worry "what if." I released it to God because it was His plan, not mine.

That was the lowest point in my life and I hope it is the lowest I ever go, unless God takes one of my other four children or six grandchildren earlier than me or Bob.

I have multiple things I value the most—health, family, forgiveness, true love and acceptance, but most especially Jesus and Jenice. I value life waiting for me in heaven. This is a stepping stone to the real life and home. This is just play-like living.

As strange as this may sound, Jenice is my mentor. I wake up every day and say, "What would Jenice do or say?" She isn't with us physically but she is with us spiritually. I also have eight to ten fantastic women in my life to laugh with me. I think laughter is important. These women have been supportive with whatever project I am involved. They are wonderful friends and have been able to get me to that other world!

I have learned that when you are involved in politics, you shouldn't think everyone is going to treat you fairly and say nice things about you.

They want to win and the best way they can win is to make you look bad. You should stay positive and stay on track of who you are and what you are trying to do. This is what I am trying to do. I always want to say, take it or leave it.

My advice to younger women is to learn to laugh at yourselves and with others. Most things are not as serious as we think they are. As a young girl, most everything was pretty serious to me. Learn to laugh with your children and at your children when they make mistakes and don't get so uptight over everything.

Diligence and persistence are important. If you believe in something and everyone in the world says you can't do it, believe in yourself. When the going gets tough, many people throw up their hands and say, "I am not going through that." We all need enough of that southern toughness, that steel magnolia down in your heart that says, "I care less what anyone else thinks. God has given me this plan and I am moving forward."

Find your strongest talent, desire or interest and focus on doing that. I believe education is important. I don't have a college degree. I made it through high school and announced that was it for me. I think continuing education is important to women going back into the work force for any reason.

Be good to yourself. Young women need to understand this. My mom used to say, "Patsy, you physically work so hard. No one is ever going to take care of you, honey, more than you. Be good to yourself." Learn to take time off, even just taking a 30 minute walk. If you don't give yourself the delights of the world, then you have nothing to give away. You are empty.

People would be surprised to know I am a perfectionist. I grew up in a time when it was ingrained in us to "do it right or don't do it at all." I run a tight ship. I am also thrilled to help people. I am not a smart lady and haven't ever worked in business, but I have been able to help people in my position as First Lady.

If Bob is not re-elected, I look forward to going back to Clay County and getting outside in my old grungy clothes and planting tulip bulbs in my yard, blowing off my sidewalk, washing my windows, washing a load of clothes and baking a chocolate pound cake. I am a good cook! I look forward to being a full time grandmother and never missing another soccer game.

If Bob is re-elected, I have improvements I want to see at the Governor's mansion. I want to finish the Hill House and open it up to the great people of Alabama. I want to work hard on the task force and the laws to protect abused children first and adults second. I want to work hard on the 1-800 number for stress, as well as the KidOne Transport for sick children. And naturally, I will continue to support my husband the next four years in his incredible plan.

Construction

LARAINE L. HECK

Laraine Heck served as the controller and corporate treasurer in a closely held family owned company in her early twenties, a remarkable achievement in the early 1960s, especially in the almost totally male and Jewish based construction supply industry in Cleveland, Ohio. Faced with enormous challenges, she eventually took over a lumber yard until its unfortunate demise.

Along the way, she became the first woman director of the Cleveland Builders Exchange, an organization over 100 years old, and was even elected President, the only woman to hold that position to this day. She was also the first woman trustee of the Ohio Lumberman's Association. In trying to make a difference in her community, she was involved with the Cleveland Mayor's Advisory Board for Women and Minority Businesses and the city's business development by lobbying in Washington, D.C.

In 1991, she won the Ernst & Young /Merrill Lynch Entrepreneur of the Year, and four years later, she was named one of the Top Twenty Women Business Owners of Northeast Ohio.

The Way I See It...

I did anything a man did… more than I needed…so I could build respect.

So Many Splinters

As far back as I can remember, I knew it was going to be a rough ride. I was nine or ten years old when "life's deal" occurred to me. I was one of six kids and my father was an alcoholic. My mom was left with three small children when he committed suicide.

I left the house, married, landed a job at a large bank, and enrolled in night school to be a lawyer someday. Then, my husband and I buried our first baby. It was a good pregnancy with a very tragic end and the first of many disappointments along the way.

I threw myself into work and was promoted pretty quickly. One of the bank's wealthy customers took a liking to me. He was foreign so he had a little less trust of people, but, for some reason, he would always come to me at the bank. We built a friendship. One day, he asked me to work for him at his construction company. I wasn't looking to change jobs, but no management opportunities existed for women at the bank. I said yes. No women worked in the construction industry either, and I knew I would be the only one at his company. I didn't care—it would be interesting.

It was not unusual that I would end up in construction supply. Even as a kid, I would do things a girl didn't do, like becoming the only girl on a guy's softball team. Others teased me, but it was okay.

As bookkeeper, I personally weighed the trucks that came in the block and gravel yard. I didn't see another woman on the job for over two years. The "john" was in the cellar, no private bathroom. There was no air conditioner or screens on the windows. My desk was near the scales, so when a truck pulled up, I had to open my window. I was dirty all the time. It was just me and those men in the hard goods business. You can't get harder than block, brick, stone and gravel. Unfortunately, the owner's son was obnoxious. I would walk to work and he would ride slowly next to me and try to talk me into getting in the car. I *had* to look for a new job.

I will never forget the interview for my next position...a very rude older gentleman blew cigar smoke in my face, yelled into the phone during our meeting and scowled at me for no apparent reason. To his surprise and mine, I was offered the job and I accepted. It paid almost double my last job.

I earned my employer's trust and although gender was very much an issue at the time, it was never an obstacle to me. I'm sure that behind closed doors, many comments were made about me and they probably called me a bitch. But never to my face. To customers, I was just an office girl, but within the company, my role was of great importance. They were very demanding, but once you were accepted and trusted, you were brought into the fold.

My acceptance at work surprised the owner's two daughters, both older than me, the most. Their father ruled with an iron hand at home and they were surprised at my success in the company because they knew their father's attitude towards women. In those days, the "Dad" owned the lumber yard and he certainly couldn't have his daughters or his wife *working* there. They were my biggest cheerleaders. A woman in management was something new. I had more clout with the owners than the other managers, but I also received the respect and support of the co-male managers. A man could not have accomplished these relationships.

The hardest part of the job was dealing with the fact that I was young and attractive. Balancing my femininity with flirtatious men was tough. Later when I had my own company, you never knew what was going to happen to you out of town...being alone with men...meeting and trying to work deals. Within a half hour of going to lunch with a big developer, he asked me to have an affair. Needless to say, I didn't get the job. Situations like that became a little disappointing and monotonous for me. I didn't have any children and they probably thought, "Who knows?" Did they truly have an interest or were they trying to break me down? I'll never know. Despite the awkward situations, constant flirtations and propositions, I was undaunted and maybe even flattered by the attention.

Being a Gentile woman in a Jewish male industry was one of the biggest issues at my former job. In the 1980s, only a few Gentiles were in the building industry in Cleveland. The business owners trusted only a handful of people. After a while, though, the rough cigar-smoking manager was leaving and recommended me to take his place.

I had come to understand that with women, it was a matter of proving competence. With men, it was assumed. The family decided to sell the company, and as lead financial person, I worked out all takeover details and was retained by the new owner. The transition was difficult, so I tendered my resignation after the contract expired.

Then, a most magical thing happened…after years of infertility, I became pregnant…a total joy and amazement!

My next surprise: the *original* owner was buying back the company after three years and asked for my help, and he wanted me to come back to work. I agreed, with stipulations. I remember lying in the hospital bed surrounded by roses and legal drafts. I would return to the business, but only as a part owner with the option of majority ownership when certain conditions existed. He was getting older and we all knew it; however, I don't believe he ever had any intention of allowing me to take over. He just wanted me to rebuild the business until his grandson could take the reins. The conditions included my ability to secure a $2 million plus line of credit, personally guaranteed. He didn't think I could do it. We became partners.

The situation went downhill fast until finally, our previously respectful relationship became out and out warfare. One time, I had to lock myself in my office as he pounded with his fist on the door yelling obscenities in front of customers and employees. I called his attorney to restrain him. Chaos ensued. I accelerated the takeover and within the next year and a half, I assumed full ownership and a credit line for $2.5 million. Raising the money included hocking everything I owned, but I did it.

For the first time this rich and powerful man with visibility in the Cleveland building industry had a major business decision go against him. Losing to a woman only added to the humiliation. I think he was astounded. A vindictive man, he caused so many problems for us. He even threatened to tell people that he was the father of my child. We almost went to court, but I knew I needed to settle. I feared that a jurist might think that an aggressive young woman stole a company away from a sweet old man.

Meanwhile, back at the lumber yard, it was business as usual. I truly struggled, running one of the largest woman-owned businesses in the city in a very difficult industry. We had many setbacks…fire, flood, tornado, rat infestation from a restaurant next door, but we moved forward.

I did anything a man did—toured the salt mines, counted $2 million of inventory in the snow, and subjected myself to down and dirty work more than I needed, so I could build respect. Some still spoke to me disrespectfully because I was a woman. I often felt mistreated.

The unions were AFL-CIO and were also Teamsters. The Cleveland unions were definitely Mafia related. When the BA's, business agents, came out to the yard, they came in their big black cars with their "piece" in their black suit jackets. You could see the guns.

I had a case that should have gone to arbitration, but the Mafia union president insisted I have dinner with him since I was a woman. I tried to get out of it, but he wouldn't let me. It was a rather routine contract and well defined, but he insisted. We went to a Sicilian restaurant for a face-to-face meeting to resolve this grievance. It was pretty amusing. He had four goons with him, all with triple chins. I sat down at the table. He said, "No, don't sit there." He sat with his back to the wall and placed me next to him. These goons surrounded us. He told the kitchen what to make and it was served in courses. It was the most wonderful Sicilian meal I have ever had in my life! I'm glad no one came in and saw me. I was alone in enemy territory, a place I would not have chosen to be. What I remember best about the evening is that the situation worked out to my favor. I don't think a man would have had to meet with the union president to resolve that issue. He was testing me. In the end, he went to prison.

After 10 years of relentless dedication and over 35 years in the construction supply business, I was confronted with a challenge that would eventually spell our demise. Our lease was not renewed. My former partner's grandson, the one being groomed to take over the lumber yard, wouldn't do it. He still held the lease. Our company suffered a tremendous setback because we had to consolidate in our other location. Sales became weak, cash reserves suffered and we began employee layoffs. We went from 50 employees to 20. In the end, I voluntarily closed the doors, a tearful day for all of us.

As for me, I woke up the next morning with no place to go, no personal identity and a horrible feeling of defeat. For those who have the courage, conviction and fortitude to even consider my journey, what happened could have been expected. I dealt with it, both good and bad.

I learned a valuable lesson: who you are, your character and ability does not change. Only the venue changes. Success goes with you no matter what you do if you apply the same principles. I have been fortunate to continue a career in project management and contract assignments for others, including medical, telecom, distribution and various industries much different than construction supply. My positive attitude, skills and experience have assured success in all these endeavors. As a volunteer counselor, I prepare all my hopeful entrepreneurs to be flexible and creative.

Recent studies have shown that young women are turning away from male-dominated positions and have the worst representation in construction and mining. According to other research, it will take women 40 years to catch up with men, so we still have not made our mark. I believe we can meet our full potential, successfully managing families and careers in male-dominated fields.

Do I think being a strong woman in an almost totally male-dominated industry was difficult and influenced the outcome? Most definitely. Missing was a support group or a good 'ole boy network. I never had an opportunity to sit with my peers over a beer or cigar and talk about business. I went to events, played in golf outings where I was the only woman, but was always treated as an outsider. Being a woman was bad enough, but I was a good golfer too. I would win my share of drives and shots and that just made matters worse. I had visibility and success, but I was never one of them, never welcomed. The men would say I "had balls." I went everywhere I wasn't welcome.

It was an uphill battle and I held my ground. I had a tremendous amount of self confidence and was so resilient, no one could break me. Weakness on the job was unacceptable. I never shed a tear. As I look back, I find that amazing.

Arts

MARILYN LOGSDON MENNELLO

Marilyn Mennello is known as the "First Lady of Tupperware," but she says she "hasn't been in any business for the last 40 years." In 1957, she was a Tupperware distributor in Pasadena, California, raising her two young daughters, Lynda and Sylvia. Five years later, she married the president of Tupperware. She traveled extensively throughout the world developing the foreign markets for Tupperware while making her permanent home in Orlando, Florida.

More widely known as the "First Lady of the Arts," she founded groups, raised millions of dollars, and sat on numerous boards. She was appointed by mayors, governors and presidents to serve on countless commissions on the arts, sciences and education. In 1976, she was co-chairman in Orange County to elect Ronald Reagan president of the United States, and later was appointed by him to serve on the National Museum Services Board of the Institute of Museum Services in Washington, D.C. and continued to serve under Presidents Bush and Clinton, thereby given the title "Honorable" before her name.

She founded two outstanding groups of volunteers. The "101 Women Volunteers" raised funds for the predecessor of the Orlando Museum of Art and garnered national attention as the most successful fundraising organization in Central Florida. The "Golden Gala Circle of Friends" raised millions for the Florida Hospital, saving countless infants' lives. These organizations will continue as her legacy.

In 1995, she became a member of the Florida Hospital Foundation Board and the next year a member of the Orlando Science Center Foundation Board.

Florida's Secretary of State, Sandra Mortham, awarded her the "Outstanding Woman Achievement Award."

She discovered Earl Cunningham, the American folk painter, while shopping in Florida with a friend in the sixties, and took on a personal quest, along with her husband Michael Mennello, to collect most of his work. Cunningham's paintings are now represented in the permanent collections of ten major museums in the U.S., including the Metropolitan Museum of Art in New York. She became the curator of this collection and often traveled lecturing on Cunningham and folk art. The City of Orlando opened the Mennello Museum of American Art in 1998, to which she and Michael gave major works of their Cunningham collection, as well as other works of folk artists. The museum has quickly become a national entity.

Movie-star beautiful, yet very approachable, Marilyn believed in hard work and dedication to a cause. "Anyone can join an organization; leading it is what matters."

Author's Note: Ms. Mennello passed away after her interview and before the publication of this book.

The Way I See It...

It is still not easy to be a single business woman. Women need to use their intelligence to understand men better.

The Great Adventurer

In 1957, I was one of the first Tupperware distributors in Pasadena, California, my hometown. My marriage had ended in divorce a few years earlier and I was raising my two young daughters, Lynda and Sylvia. My girls were my constant working companions. They helped me pack materials for delivery and went with me to clients' homes. They would often get bored waiting in the car while I made my rounds with Tupperware. Child care was out of the question…it was non-existent.

I was a Girl Scout leader, drove carpool, took my daughters to music, tennis and dance lessons, sewed their clothes, and did artwork for their school projects. Raising young children alone was a challenge for any woman in the 1950s, but I learned to maneuver pretty well.

Women also didn't have much status in business when I started, but Tupperware gave them a chance to be a star at night and still take care of the children when their husbands went to work. They could have fun with other women at the same time they made money.

Five years after I became a distributor, I married the president of the Tupperware Company, Hamer F. Wilson. Mr. Tupper, the founder of Tupperware, hired my husband as the international president of Tupperware Home Parties. For the next 14 years, I traveled with him around the world marketing the Tupperware brand. We worked with managers and distributors, conducting research and developing foreign markets. It was an exciting time. Free enterprise was at its best and Tupperware and Coca Cola set the standard. I became a pioneer, paving the way in parts unknown with my husband.

In 1957, Tupperware came out with the CARS program and managers were given cars. I went to Australia to set up the Tupperware Company and in Tasmania, not one out of ten women had ever owned a car. No one ever left the house. It was a man's world entirely. I have a feeling it must still be.

My entry into the man's world back then is the same as it is today…the "power of men" versus "very little power for women." It was a corporate world I walked into. However, I always enjoyed working with men *because* they had the power.

Rexall Drug and Chemical bought Tupperware in 1960 from Mr. Tupper. Rexall's name was changed to Dart Industries, of which Justin Dart was president. Most of the corporate officers of this company eventually became Ronald Reagan's cabinet. That gives you a little idea of the power they held. Of course, Mr. Dart would not allow women on the board. With all things equal, I would have been a logical choice as a board member.

My time with Tupperware was over when my marriage ended. I haven't been in any business since, except when I owned a small dress shop with a partner. It didn't make it. I have just been a volunteer for 40 years who loves art.

When I divorced my husband, women looked at me differently. Their husbands were impressed with me but it was off putting to women. It is still not easy to be a single business woman. Women are fearful of each other. Their attitude wasn't upsetting to me, just interesting and factual. You can be young, successful and divorced, and the men will be very accepting and proud of you, admiring your success, but other women don't necessarily feel that way about you. Divorce was sometimes worse than death back then.

Legally, women had a chance for a better divorce settlement before the National Organization for Women era. In the 1950s, when you divorced, you were unprepared and thrown into the unknown, but at least you might have been taken care of financially. But with liberation, women who were dying to get out of the house went to work, no longer satisfied with just being Mrs. Housewife. Work gave them an excuse to be free every day, something that they had wanted for years. Families soon discovered they needed more goods for their homes and couldn't survive without two salaries. That's when the family life crashed.

I say let men bear most of the responsibility. I don't want to worry with what they do. Their hormones are better suited. War and sports are good examples of how different we are from men. Their whole way of thinking is different...kill them, get out there, put them down...it's just a different attitude than women. Let them have it. Women can't stop them. Procreation is a man's job. Their hormones get into areas women would never go. I am thankful for men, not against them.

A man can live with a woman more easily than a woman can live with a man, but it does no good to *dislike* men. Women need to use their intelligence to understand men better. They should have a course on the male psyche in school. Most teenage boys only have sex on their mind. Today, sex is only pleasure...there is no emotional tie like in my day. Girls are ridiculous to give themselves away.

If I were president of the United States, I would make every high school graduating boy and girl spend one year in the military, getting a psychological evaluation, learning how to treat the opposite sex, gaining etiquette, manners, discipline and skills. After that, they can go to college.

Young women need to look at their skills, know their dreams and go for it. I raised my daughters to become self sufficient and strong enough to make it on their own. I was adamant they attend college, able to make a living on their own. I wanted them to understand it's a man's world, but there are ways to fit in.

Now, I wonder if women *really do* have it easier than women from my era, the early pioneers. There are more interesting jobs now. If I could live my life over, I would be a food critic and do a cookbook. I love cooking and I love recipes. The food industry is fascinating to me.

I have had a great adventure and I believe happiness is all a state of mind. We make our own happiness. God plays a great part in our lives. When life doesn't seem fair, if you believe that God is leading you, you will understand later why it was best for you.

Civil Rights

ROXCY O'NEAL BOLTON

Roxcy Bolton's former house at 1302 Alhambra Circle was designated as a Florida Heritage Site on August 26, 1999. It was on that same day in 1920 that women in the United States received the right to vote. Meetings held at Ms Bolton's house had resulted in the first hearings on the Equal Rights Amendment before Congress in 1970.

This same day, August 26, in 1972, President Nixon declared a Women's Equality Day predominantly due to Ms Bolton's work and perseverance.

Born in 1926, she is Florida's Pioneer Feminist and the founder of Florida NOW, serving as its national vice president in 1969. She founded the first Rape Treatment Center in the country in Miami; Women in Distress, the first women's shelter in Florida; Crime Watch, to help stem crime against women; Women's Park and the Women's History Gallery in Miami, another first in the country.

She is the only feminist to receive the Miami Herald *"Spirit of Excellence Award," and she was inducted into the Florida Women's Hall of Fame in 1984 in recognition of her accomplishments for the cause of women's rights. The "Roxcy Bolton Collection" is in the Florida Department of Archives, which includes the red suit she wore to the swearing in ceremony of U.S. Supreme Court Justice Sandra Day O'Conner.*

Her photo is outside the governor's office in Tallahassee.

The Way I See It...

Aim high and persevere and never let anything get in your way.

Warriors Don't Cry

Eleanor Roosevelt said to me, "Roxcy, never let a dead end street stop you from where you're going." She also told me, "You must do the things you think you cannot do." She had just given me a real task—do the things you cannot do? Many times I have felt worn down and gained strength from her words…the way she expressed it to me and the way she spoke. I have her picture. I look at it often and remember what strength, what courage she gave me. Whatever my challenge, I had to keep going, no matter how hard. You have to keep your head, that's for sure.

In the early 1960s, I went shopping at Burdines Department Store in Miami with my little babies. I dashed upstairs to get a bite of lunch. It was just rush, rush when you had little children. A long line of women waited for a table while the men's section had empty tables. No men were standing in line! That really pissed me off as I stood in line, anxious, impatient and aggravated.

At home, I called the store's vice president in charge of personnel. "This separate seating for men and women is intolerable. I want to talk to you about it." We set up a meeting.

I called a friend of mine who was a black female lawyer for the Coast Guard. I wanted her to go with me. She said, "I guess if I could march for civil rights, I could march up to Burdines." We met at the front door. She looked at me thoughtfully. "Roxcy, you be the heavy."

He invited us into his office and I wasted no time. "We are here to change the policy of seating."

He was incredulous. "But Mrs. Bolton, we have done this for so long!"

I wouldn't budge. "I am telling you that people will like the change. You have 30 days."

"Or?"

"Or, I will stand in front of your store and pass out the best tuna sandwiches in town and boycott people from eating in your restaurant since you don't let women have the same privileges as men." I could tell by his body language that it concerned him. "Within 30 days of today, I want a letter stating you will not continue the policy of seating men and making women stand in line. Men and women sleep together, why can't they eat together?" When I said that, he swallowed so hard, I thought he was going to swallow his teeth! It was really something.

Within 30 days, I received the letter. It is in the archives of the Roxcy Bolton Collection in Tallahassee.

Following the meeting with Burdine's, the same thing happened at Jordan Marsh Department Store. After they sent a letter stating their change in policy, I went to lunch with my husband to check it out. When the dining room receptionist greeted us, I asked, "What happened? You don't have a men's dining room anymore?"

She said, "No! The government made us change it."

My husband leaned over and said to me, "Without honor in your own country." I'm sure that was the story Jordan Marsh told their employees. They didn't want to say *feminists* made them change.

We made a difference...we made it better.

The Equal Rights Amendment was passed by calling Florida's Senator Gurney almost every day for months. Finally he agreed to come to my house. We asked him to hold hearings on the amendment in Washington and received his agreement to work it out of committee. That will live on forever. Senator Birch Bayh was a friend of mine on the ERA subcommittee. He had been to my home too. The day it passed, he called me from the senate floor. Of course, it didn't pass the states. That's unfortunate...I don't know if I'll live long enough to see that happen.

The three things I want most in life have not happened yet. I want to be a grandmother. I want to see the passage of the ERA by the states. I want a woman in the White House. I'm batting zero. But I have always aimed high and persevered, and I have never let anything get in my way.

People often ask me, "Why don't you like men?"

I reply, "I love men."

My concern isn't love or hate—it is equality. When almost every meeting is predominantly composed of men, they feel that they have an edge.

Their viewpoints constantly overshadow everything else. "Why do you want to do that? You always want something for women. We don't hear this from any other woman. We never hear anybody talking about women being discriminated against because we don't have a woman on such and such board." They have a way of putting women down, trying to make them look foolish.

I spoke before the Metro Dade Commission trying to establish the Commission on the Status of Women and even some of the *women* opposed it. When women take a stand against you because you're trying to do something *for women, it hurts.*

Nobody today would have the nerve to ask me, "Why are you doing that for women?"

I have been on the streets with the police to see how women fared. I saw them sleeping on the street, by a tree, in the cemetery, in a cardboard box. It was heart wrenching to see what was happening to our women with all the wealth, power and beauty in downtown Miami. I founded Women in Distress, the first women's rescue shelter in Florida. At least they had a place to go. We managed to feed everybody, no matter how many came.

I remember Mae, who slept and eventually died on the Methodist church steps. She was going to be buried at the pauper's cemetery and city officials wouldn't allow anyone to go to that gravesite. I said, "You'll have to change your policy because I'm a taxpayer." I called the Mayor's office and told his aide to instruct the board that I could attend her funeral. The next day, I jumped the fence with flowers from my house. There was Mae's grave, a cardboard casket sitting in a foot of water because it had rained. The Methodist minister, would you believe it, reached over to take my flowers and said, "I'll put them on Mae's grave."

I said, "Oh, no you won't. I'll do that." Somehow the Associated Press got that story and it went all over the country—a picture of me putting flowers on Mae's grave. Our senator wrote me a letter thanking me for caring about Mae. The last I saw of her was in that cardboard box.

Rape was rampant in Miami—practically in broad daylight. Men had to walk their secretaries to their cars. The problem was generally ignored by the police. I led a march down Flagler Street protesting. I expected 50 to come and 100 showed up. To me, it was like having 10,000 marching. At that time women didn't consider protesting—we weren't geared up for marching. A policeman kept pace with me at the head of the group. "Are these the only women in Dade County opposed to rape?" His comment meant, "Who cares? What's the big problem?"

I said, "Is your mother or sister or wife here?"

You do what you have to do… we marched. We finally got our Rape Treatment Center. Again, we made a difference.

A friend of mine at the Equal Employment Opportunity Commission, EEOC, in Atlanta called me. "Roxcy, we've opened an office in Miami but the director is only hiring men."

I called the director and tried to be diplomatic. "I'm concerned…my friend has told me you're only hiring men."

The director replied, "I do have one black man."

"Well, black comes in two sexes," I reminded him.

It was odd that this agency had a mandate to promote equal opportunity and all the investigators were men. I called my friend and television star at Channel 10, Molly Turner. She wanted to go with me to see him. Of course, she brought her camera and we didn't alert him we were coming. When we walked in, he was shocked. He had this big, grand fine office. He looked at Molly and said, "Molly Turner, what's a nice woman like you doing here with Roxcy Bolton?" It was on the evening news and I rather enjoyed that.

I also went to see the president of the University of Miami with my bedroll and a picnic basket, in case I had to wait a while to see him. He had avoided me long enough. I wanted more women as department heads and equal salaries for men and women doing the same work. I called Molly Turner for that unannounced visit too. Getting press for my efforts always boosted the cause.

One day, I received a frantic call from a mother who, along with other mothers, was nursing her baby in a park in downtown Miami. She was in a panic because the police were threatening to arrest them. I called the Attorney General.

He came on the line. "Roxcy, is this really an emergency?"

I calmly made my point. "Mr. Attorney General, did your mother nurse you? The police are going to arrest some women in a park in Miami because they are nursing their babies, giving their babies life support. Will you help us?"

"Yes, I will. Right now." He called the city attorney and the mayor of Miami.

Shortly, I received another call from the women at the park. "Roxcy, all of a sudden, the police just left!" I loved it. Those mothers were on network television and the story landed on the front page, above the fold, of the *Miami Herald*.

Again, we made a difference.

In 1979, I badgered the Hurricane Center until they agreed to stop naming hurricanes only after women. It was always a scary headline in the paper and I didn't like it one bit...*Hurricane Mary Kills 7 People...Linda Ruins Town* or some such devastating announcement. The first time I went to see Dr. Johanssen, the head of the center, I didn't get anywhere. His personnel laughed at me and thought it was funny. They made jokes; it was disheartening. The second time I went, I told Dr. Johanssen I had a solution ..."We'll name hurricanes for U.S. senators."

He said, "You would embarrass our senators nationally and internationally?"

I had my answer ready. "You don't mind degrading and humiliating women, but you're reluctant about senators? I don't understand."

The third time I had yet another solution. "We'll name them for birds."

He said, "Then you'd have the Audubon Society on my back."

Frustration set in. "You don't care what happens to women and their image; you just care about senators and birds."

It took about two years to change it. Again, we made a difference.

The truth will set you free...it just takes twice as long.

People ask why I didn't run for public office. I didn't have the patience. My interests are women, employee and black rights. I couldn't listen to some zoning lawyer tell a bunch of lies or to some damn fool thing that's not good for the city. I am not suited to be a public official. Rather than put myself through that, I chose not to run. Some city leaders have retaliated against me over the years, but, in the last analysis, it doesn't matter. My work for justice and equality will outlast any of the small minds. Small minded views sadden me, but I am not going to dwell on that. I like who I am and I am comfortable with my journey and my approach. I'm not everybody's cup of tea. You've got to have a strong mind to understand what I do at times. But I must have done something right to be in the Hall of Fame. As time marches on, your work is remembered differently.

If you have truth on your side, never let them beat you down. Never let them see you cry. Warriors don't cry.

"We aim to give a wake-up call to businesses, to alert them to the fact that the next fair-headed boy of their organization just might be a woman."

—Elizabeth Dole
Former U.S. Senator of North Carolina
& former CEO of American Red Cross

JOAN HULL

Joan Hull admits that the lively part of her life started at age 40 when she joined the newly formed New York City chapter of NOW, the National Organization for Women, in 1967. She is famous for her heroine role in the "shareholder proposal movement," which resulted in the appointment of women to the boards of directors of major corporations, including her own company, Celanese. Gulf Oil, Exxon, Sears, Roebuck, I.B.M. and Xerox soon followed. She landed on the business pages of the New York Times *and* Wall Street Journal *and was generally known, in her words, as a "pain in the neck."*

Mild mannered with a no-nonsense approach, this tireless champion of women's rights forged a path for change throughout her career.

The Way I See It...

Women have the leisure of choosing where they want to work in planning their career. They should keep in mind that opportunities are no different today for men and women.

First Blood

In 1949, I graduated from Skidmore College.

In 1969, I filed a sex discrimination complaint against my company with the New York State Division of Human Rights. My company was called Celanese, a major public corporation with over 65,000 employees in the textile industry. When I started at Celanese in 1963, women shared offices with men who were doing the same jobs. We became acutely aware of where *we* were and where *they* were. The company gave them different titles and of course, they were paid more. We were sensitive to that. The women were doing the bulk of the paperwork while the men had no paperwork requirements. Every time management changed supervisors, a woman would train the next man that came into the department. We didn't experience any movement or advancement within the company.

The women's movement was coming in strong. NOW was founded in 1966 to promote equal rights for women. Even before I joined NOW in 1967, I wanted to move ahead and have more responsibility and decision making. Women who joined NOW all had an issue, whether it was divorce, child care, promotions, etc. Mine was employment. I knew my rights and no one from Celanese belonged to NOW but me. New York had one of the strongest NOW chapters because we were the media capital. Many remarkable women joined and our voices were beginning to be heard.

I read about the Civil Rights Act passed by Congress in 1964 and I knew it would become active in 1965. Yet, nothing happened in our company. No announcement, nothing telling us about opportunities, for women *or* men.

I called my friend who was director of personnel in a large corporation in New York City. "What are you doing about the Civil Rights Act?" She said nothing was going on at her company either. A big alarm went off in my head. I asked if she wanted to join NOW. She said no, it would be seen as company disloyalty. She didn't have huge career aspirations— maybe she would get her boss' job in 15 years. She was content and well paid with a good job.

I started asking questions of my supervisor. I wanted to see my personnel reviews and discuss my future. I also wanted his job! I asked him what the company was going to do about equal employment and poked pretty soft questions to get an idea of where he personally stood. I was careful, never aggravating and never using any threats. I wanted him to know I was interested in moving up and gently asked him how many men were being moved around. I got nowhere and I was out of options.

I filed my sex discrimination complaint because I asked him for a reclassification and salary adjustment and was denied. My male associate had fewer responsibilities, less work, a higher classification, and was making $4,000 more a year. I had trained four bosses; saw 19 male associates receive job changes; saw men hired from the outside at a higher salary to do my job; and had no indication that these shenanigans would ever change. There was no time left.

I approached other women in the company to explain the new law—it provides equal opportunity for employment. I framed a statement and sent it to the personnel department and most of the women signed it.

At that time, secretaries were classified, graded and compensated according to the pecking order of their boss. Women were never told how their supervisor rated their annual performance review. Maternity was not treated as a temporary disability and jobs were not held for women who took maternity leave. Company sponsored training was not offered to women. The title, "Director of" was limited to men. Women were not encouraged to develop their career. No women were in the sales department. Men held all line managerial positions and women were paid less at the same level and often had more education.

One of our vice presidents was quoted in a national magazine. "A big problem is finding qualified women to promote with higher responsibilities. More than 40 percent of the people who work for me are women and I am sympathetic with their desire to become managers, but the plain fact is that it is difficult to find qualified women at the managerial level."

When women were seeking to move up, the executives would respond: "Will your husband permit you to be away for a week-long training course?" Or, "Our mill customers do not want a woman calling on them."

In the meantime, my case of discrimination was conciliated and I was promoted. Later in 1972, I filed again because in downsizing, the company demoted me. This time, there was *not* a satisfactory conciliation and the company continued to show a lack of progress for women. As a result, a class action suit was filed in federal court in 1973. The court notified all the women who previously signed my petition and gave them an opportunity to be in or out. Half of them opted out. They were afraid of losing their jobs and being out of sorts with the management.

No one wins this type of case, but the company did start to make strides in promoting women and I was delighted with the progress. The class action suit dragged on for 12 years. It seemed to go on forever. Women at the *New York Times, Newsweek, Time*, area banks and businesses began discussing and pushing for equality in their careers and they too were successful. The Equal Employment Opportunity Commission, EEOC, intervened in my class action in support of the claims made. However, Celanese immediately hired two past EEOC officers, one a former officer of NOW and the other the past Chair of the Commission, to discredit the class action. Unfortunately, they were successful.

To keep pressure on the company, I submitted three of NOW's stockholder proposals to be voted on at the annual meetings in 1974, '75 and '76. The proposals asked for women to be appointed to the board, cumulative voting, and full reporting of the company's affirmative action progress. We told the *New York Times* female financial reporter about the event and asked her to cover it. She brought a photographer. Celanese was not prepared for the successful barrage of feminist groups that showed up. The Interfaith Council on Corporate Responsibility even had three different groups of nuns properly dressed in their habits!

The Chairman of the Board of Celanese lost his composure, "We aren't going to fill a job with a woman as a token."

He was chided for his "seeming antagonism" to the women stockholders and his attempt to "scapegoat the women here." Press coverage was more about the dialog than the business of the meeting. The *Times* reporter told me it was the best feminist event she had ever covered. The *Wall Street Journal* reporter mirrored her report. The next day, the officers pinned a sign on their suit lapels that read, "GYB." Translation: Guard Your Balls. Within two years, the company appointed two women to the board.

An officer of Gulf Oil Company attended the Celanese meeting because his annual meeting was the following week and a NOW member had submitted similar proposals to be considered. He anxiously asked the NOW member if their "group" would be attending the Gulf meeting. She said they were not. Regardless, after the Gulf meeting, the corporation immediately appointed a woman to their board. A few weeks later, NOW proposals were voted on at the Sears annual meeting.

At Celanese, the tendency was to treat females as objects, girls. But once I filed my first lawsuit in 1969, they started to treat me as a competitor. I was taken seriously and that's what I wanted. Before my decision to file, I spoke with a NOW lawyer. She said it would be very rough and gave me an idea of what to expect. I thought about everything she said and decided my attitude would have to be very open.

My relationship with Celanese men completely changed. I was now seen as a person, not some little fluke. I was simply a down-to-earth person, competing in the business world. Some of them shared my anger; they felt they had been overlooked too. Every employee has that feeling of not being appreciated or recognized, but this was anger stemming from jealousy: "The government is helping her. She can file suit because she's supposed to have opportunities." Men don't readily open up their feelings, but it was a sense I had. Even more expressive were the Jewish and Italian men. They felt pushed aside. Some were department heads, but it was rare you would see an officer or a vice president. The top executives in upper management were WASPS, White Anglo Saxon Protestants. They were members of the Princeton Club, the Harvard Club, or the Yale Club. I had a card to the Princeton Club too. I didn't fear them. I walked tall. I smiled. I didn't wear it on my sleeve.

If anybody wanted to know what was happening, I would tell them. I didn't speak about it—they had to ask me, though almost no one did. It was business as usual. Maybe they were afraid.

The company eventually removed a man from a job and gave it to me. This showed people there was some justification in my complaint. It probably gave the women a boost because they could see things were happening. The men began to realize that the women were true competitors. It wasn't going to be white men only.

I was never conscious of making history. I thought everybody would get behind the movement. That wasn't the case. Women were afraid to stick their neck out. They would call me from within the company. Secretaries who had been promoted and now worked on the corporate level were under pressure to retire or quit because their boss had spotted a young girl he wanted for a replacement. All they had to do was walk across the street in midtown Manhattan to the wage and hour department and talk to an intake person about their rights. They wouldn't do it.

I had to be careful because I was a little leery that the company would stage an employee to call me and record the information I gave her. I didn't want to appear too legal. I walked a tightrope.

Women today enjoy so many rights in the workplace, but still the challenge exists for equality and *understanding*. Women often don't have the pressure of economics to support a family. Society does not expect them to bear that burden. Their husbands will. As a result, women can follow their interests...plan and chart a course...or even start a business...something entrepreneurial. Or they can take a low level job just to learn about a company, knowing they can move up. This usually results in happier women than men. Society expects men to have an excellent job, get good pay and be able to support a family. Men usually start in higher company positions. They don't learn the systems from the ground up like women do. When I go into a bank, I don't like to go to a male teller. If I have a problem, I go to a woman. I know she started lower in the bank than he did and she knows the system and how to correct any errors.

Look at your friends and families...you see that girls are outperforming the boys. Look at the Kennedy family. Robert Kennedy's daughter was a lieutenant governor. Caroline Kennedy was way ahead of her brother. There is no difference in intelligence between men and women, but women are *using* it now. This reflects negatively on men. Jobs and promotions don't automatically go to white males. In my day, people actively sought out men for all jobs and promotions. Virtually one half of the workforce was ignored. You run out of good people fast that way.

Retail

LORRAINE MILLER

With $1,000 in her pocket, Lorraine Miller founded Cactus & Tropicals, a garden store and plant maintenance company. Starting in 1975, she grew her company to a multi-million dollar business and sold it.

Along the way, she founded the Utah Association of Women Business Owners and won the Woman of Achievement Award from the Salt Lake YWCA. She won many more awards, but one catapulted her business to another level: the National Small Business Person of the Year by the Small Business Administration.

The Way I See It...

Sometimes we are our own worst enemies. If we stand together, many of us can rise. If we speak against each other, we can only blame ourselves for our failures.

Always Speaking Out

I'm a war baby. I always felt I had to fight for my very existence.

When my father came home from WWII, he arrived with an American dream to build a printing business and pass it on to his firstborn son. Guaranteeing the Miller gene would survive. It was a common attitude that male children were innately better than female children. My brother was told at an early age that the business would be his. I knew this and didn't question it. It seemed normal. Still, I wanted that printing business. It was called Lorraine Press! Unfortunately, it wasn't even a contest. No possibility of even a partnership existed with my brother. The ancient law of primogeniture prevailed. Being a girl automatically made me a second class citizen and nothing I could do would prove my competency.

I had two sisters. Those of us who went to college did so in spite of my father. He didn't think it was important for girls to get a college education. He was focused on my older brother. I was angry and felt the injustice. But in many ways, I am glad for that experience. It drove me to work on issues of justice and equality all my life. Since I grew up in an environment where I had no marketable value, I jokingly say I was successful because I had to prove to my father and others that I could succeed despite their attitudes. If only I could have been a boy, I would have had the world by a string. I don't want to sound whiny—I would rather cast the voice that "here was discrimination and I spoke out." Sometimes my voice gets me in trouble.

My father faced discrimination being Jewish, so he told my brother when he left for college not to tell anyone that his father was Jewish. He wouldn't be accepted by a good fraternity if he did. I was born with a different view. My brother would lie about his heritage, but I never would. I was proud of it.

My mother was always supportive of me...treated me like I was intelligent. She was very proud of my civil rights work as a Vista volunteer after I finished college. She called me her "senator." She didn't go to college and felt she had lost out on opportunities.

When I was young, she would say, "Modulate your kisser." We weren't supposed to be aggressive or speak out when we saw things happening—but I always did, even as a young girl. I learned about the cruelty of prejudice at a very early age when another child said to me, "I can't play with you because you're not Mormon."

As I ventured into the world of business, both Dad and I would be surprised to discover that his gift for entrepreneurialism could be inherited by either sex. In 1975, with $1,000 in my pocket, I opened a plant shop. One Mother's Day morning, it just came to me. I had a vision of operating a plant shop. I had no money and no plant knowledge but I guess I had a lot of chutzpah, because I jumped in my car and before the day came to an end, I had found a boarded up building to rent. I ran an ad in the paper. "Wandering Jews looking for a home." I was on my way.

Salt Lake hosted a conference for International Women's Year not long after I started my business. About 20 of my women's association friends attended. We put forth a resolution that said, "Support Women Owned Businesses." It was voted down! I turned to one of the women sitting next to me who had voted against us and asked her why. She said, "You women should be home raising families, not having businesses." Her response was my first realization that I was stepping into a world that wasn't welcoming. Even now in Utah, they feel that women should be housekeepers, at home raising children with the man bringing home the bread.

My business grew and developed and started winning awards. I worked seven days a week for 12 years. I never took a vacation. If it was a holiday and my business was closed, I would sleep all day. I was afraid of failure. It drove me to success. I couldn't let the stigma that my father had attached to me cause my failure. The building I rented had an apartment upstairs and I moved in. At night, if I looked down and saw someone peering in the window, I would dash down the stairs to make a sale. Every penny I made went back into the business.

In three years, I had enough money to purchase a delivery van. I roamed around the truck lot and was standing near a shiny red cargo van visualizing my logo emblazoned on its side when a salesman greeted me.

I told him, "I'd like to test drive this one."

He stared at me, incredulous, and said, "But ma'am, are you the decision maker?"

I said, "Yes, I am, go get the keys, please."

After he went behind the curtain and did his little credit check, he came back and declared, "Oh, you're good 'people.'"

I had a funny feeling I had morphed into a being of both sexes and the male part of me put the whole of me in good standing with his point of view. Constantly, things like that happened.

Loan officers were always surprised to find that a woman had collateral or a down payment. Since my business grew so quickly, I had to go to a bank. My accountant offered to introduce me and go on the appointment so he could "talk to the numbers." I gratefully accepted the intervention but I felt diminished to the age of a ten year old. They talked about me as if I wasn't there. I felt like a good girl who deserved a pat on the head. My accountant rhapsodized about my hard work and on occasion, they would look at me and smile or nod. I was humiliated, but to be honest, I had no defense. I had been focused on creating a nifty garden center, not on tracking percentages or bottom lines. I didn't understand financial statements and I couldn't talk the language. On the other hand, I didn't deserve their condescension. Needless to say, after that experience, I learned everything I could know about financials. I also found a new accountant and a different bank and was approved for a $50,000 SBA loan.

Time passed and that loan was nearly paid off. Again, I went to the bank, proudly able to discuss my financials without help, and applied for a new SBA loan. To my amazement, I was turned down.

Right about that time, Karen Shepherd, who later became one of Utah's state representatives, started a women's newspaper called *Network*. One of their journalists called me for an interview about my business and I told her I had just been turned down for a SBA loan. I was very critical of the banker because I had good credit and a solid loan payment history. I felt discriminated against. One of my closest friends had just been told by her bank, "You've got pretty legs, but it's not going to get you any money."

The *Network* story was passed around and all the bankers had a good laugh over my comments, since it was clearly out of prejudice, but their smiles turned to frowns when they realized the facts in the article didn't look good for bankers. The head of the bankers association called another woman in my association. "Lorraine needs to apologize for this and if she doesn't, it's going to be difficult for more women to get loans." A threat!

I was outraged. "I will not apologize. I told the truth in my interview and if an apology needs to be made, it should come from the banker who rejected my loan."

I was shocked that she agreed with the banker. A few weeks went by and a competing bank called and I got the loan. The banker that turned me down was fired.

I couldn't believe that women were upset with me! They felt the best way to get loans was to cow tow. It was humiliating and shameful. I felt I had to speak out.

The woman who said I needed to apologize later confessed that I was right. She was the bank's interior designer and was afraid she would lose her job if she didn't speak against me. It took her 35 years to tell me the truth. It was very difficult for her to do.

The greatest consequence of all this was the initiation of a series of Bankers Roundtables. Women quickly became more sophisticated in their business approach and the bankers suddenly had a huge, new market.

It is hard to be in the lead of a battle. When you are the point person, you get beat up and don't always get the support you need. Sometimes we are our own worst enemies. If we stand together, many of us can rise. If we speak against each other, we can only blame ourselves for our failures.

Men were always surprised at my success and a little too condescending. My voice was nothing. Sometimes, I had to catch their attention. I never took on a membership to the Utah Nurserymen's Association and they never invited me to join them. In my eyes, they were a bunch of unsophisticated farmers who had never reached out to women. Not one of them ever acknowledged that I made our industry proud. It was the women's groups that gave me accolades, not my industry. Many of them have since failed or gone bankrupt.

Many years later, I was nominated for the National Small Business Person of the Year. I was especially pleased to be nominated by my banker, a man that looked at his clients as people, not as one sex or another. I won the award, only the third woman in 31 years. It was huge for my business. The next morning, my parking lot and greenhouses were full of people waiting to congratulate me.

I kicked up my business to the next level. I was invited to be on the board of the chamber and to give speeches. I became the chairperson of the Utah delegation at the White House Conference on Small Business. I sold my company in 2002 to a man who wants to clone it and franchise it throughout the west. He gave me a business card with the word "Founder" on it.

When I was younger and saw what was going on with men, I wished that I could have been a boy. Not now. I'm so happy being a woman. We changed banking, corporate boards and government because we kept pushing against the system. Look at what women have done, what an individual can do. The world is a better place, more open and inclusive. We no longer allow ourselves to step back and be put down.

And, by the way, my father was proud of me too.

Finance

"In my day, women couldn't enter the Detroit Athletic Club's front door. The members would go to a side door to allow you entrance. I was so anxious to get into that club, I would have come through the coal chute. I do not rest on ceremony."

—*Catherine Flynn*
Entrepreneur, Detroit, Michigan

MARJORIE J. WEBER

When Marjorie Weber started her career in New York City no other women with influence were in her field. Hired as an administrative assistant at Sonnenblick-Goldman Corporation in 1964, she ended up running the well known investment banking firm until 1978. She then moved to Miami as president and co-owner of one of the largest real estate and mortgage companies in South Florida, Florida Fidelity.

Spanning over 43 years, her experience and knowledge has been utilized in the non-profit sector as well. She was a United Way Agency director and chairperson, served on the Miami Beach Blue Ribbon Art Deco Panel, the Miami Beach Botanical Garden Conservatory, the City of Miami Beach Loan Review Board, and was a Founding Director of the Dade County Not-For-Profit Organization, providing grants to the art community.

The Way I See It...

We're always playing roles with people. I don't mean to sound manipulative but it happens. The people you can't manipulate, you stay away from.

Manipulation is a tough word, but we're getting the best out of people while making them happy too.

My Way in Manhattan

I had a role in changing the skylines of both Manhattan and Miami.

I laugh today when younger people in the industry refer to me as a legend. I don't know if I should be flattered or insulted. I have stories to tell from the past, and even today working pro-bono, I face confrontations due to the differences between the sexes...because I am a woman. I have never learned to accept the fact that my colleagues considered me a tough broad. I thought they were talking about someone else. I was shocked and upset because that was not my self image. What I consider tenacity, others might consider stubbornness. I see myself as just a woman with a traditional upbringing in the 1930s who found herself in the heart of Manhattan's financial world and somehow survived.

I always kept a low profile, but was involved in enormous real estate projects. Men were braggadocios; I was not. When I started, absolutely no women were in a position of power in commercial real estate, finance or mortgage banking. To my credit, I never tried to play a man's role, never ever. I was fortunate that I was associated with very powerful men. Just being with them gave me credibility. I took advantage of it.

I was not a strident follower of the women's movement, maybe a bit indifferent. How could I be strident about women's rights from nine to five and then turn into a sexual siren after work? I was a mother of two young children—disqualifying me from the after five option, but I couldn't be Jekyll and Hyde in the same day. I supported the principals of the feminist movement, but I rejected many of their methods. I chose to be supportive of my male colleagues. I was not their adversary...I was their accomplice. Besides, men weren't threatened by my competence since I was *not* competition from their vantage point.

An advantage of being a pioneer was taking part within the first generation of women executives entering a man's profession. Unknowingly, I was a crusader for the next generation. Unfortunately, I didn't benefit from others who had "been through it."

I joined Sonnenblick-Goldman, S/G, in the mid 1960s. Many of the firm's mature men had never worked with women colleagues and it was hard for them to accept women in the workplace who did not order lunch or take dictation. They addressed me as "honey" or "sweetie." A chill ran through my body and I would swallow hard…it was offensive to me. So I came up with my standard reply: "The only man who calls me honey pays my bills." I never had to repeat it to the same man.

My first boss, Sid Troy at S/G, hired me on my first interview. He had just lost his wife and he needed help with home matters…his kids…his house. I wasn't high brow; I made myself valuable. Many women feminists wouldn't touch those jobs. They weren't going to play those roles. Perhaps in some industries, you could get away with it, but not in mine. I played those roles, but I stood my ground too.

We're always playing roles with people. I don't mean to sound manipulative, but we are. The people you can't manipulate, you stay away from. Manipulation is a tough word, but we're getting the best out of people while making them happy too. I had financial skills, but if the company needed to redecorate the offices, who was it going to be? I had enough common sense to get it done. I'm sorry to say that men didn't know how to do the everyday mundane things that had to be done. Women multi-task and men get going in one direction and can't see the rest of the world.

After working at S/G for three years, my big break came when the sales manager unexpectedly resigned. Bill Stern, one of the partners, asked me to take over. As office manager, I was earning exactly one half of what the sales manager was being paid: $18,000 vs. $36,000 per year. I asked Bill for confirmation that I would get $36,000 too and he informed me that I would only get a slight increase in pay.

The discussion was held in the corridor outside his office and close to mine, usually crowded with people. He said, "You should not expect to be paid the same because your predecessor was a man with a family and you are a woman."

I felt instant rage! I was embarrassed to show such strong emotion, but I was furious. I had no smart retort to his proposal. My eyes filled with tears and I could only get out a few guttural words between my sobs, "But I'm the mother of two children with financial responsibility!"

Neither of us knew how to respond to my sobbing. I was left standing there.

I could not believe my response. I spent all night filled with anger towards him and shame at myself for losing control. The salary offer was not the major issue…I was enraged at his attitude towards women.

The following day, he confirmed that I would get the raise I had requested. To this day, I am not sure why he changed his mind. I admit that I never overcame my dislike for this man who naturally assumed that because I was a woman, I should earn less than a man. I felt no glory in having obtained the raise in such a feminine fashion, but I believe the tears were an effective tool. He was known to be insensitive to everything but transactions. Maybe because I responded like a "woman," I won the day. I never discussed it with anyone because I was too embarrassed.

I was about to manage 15 extraordinary men, which would grow to 99 in 14 offices over the years. Often, my "woman's intuition" would be called upon by the executive vice president to make final decisions on hiring.

On Christmas Eve, 1973, when the market crashed, I fired seven men at one time. It broke my heart. Realizing I might be fired too, I went into the chairman's office and offered to take a cut in salary. He was so embarrassed, what could he do? I told him if he cut my salary, I would go on commission in sales. He agreed.

Instead of a management position, I jumped into a sales position. The senior vice president asked me if I was ready to work from 5 *p.m.* to 9 *p.m.* instead of 9 *a.m.* to 5 *p.m.* He felt the only way I would be successful as a broker would be to entertain the bankers at night. I just shrugged it off. I ended up making real money…a lot of money…over six figures. Larry Silverstein, owner of the World Trade Center complex in New York City, became one of my clients. He was a young man, one of my contemporaries at the time I dealt with real estate financing.

In the early 1970s, few women were in sales positions. For this reason, they had considerable advantage over their male counterparts. A woman could decide on a target client and almost always be assured of getting the appointment. A pleasant female phone voice created an aura of curiosity. A man wanted to know about the face and the body that went with the voice. He would never admit to this fact, but there is no doubt it played a part in getting that first visit. It was unusual for me to fail in getting an appointment. But as more women entered the profession, the window of opportunity shrank and the element of curiosity diminished.

Sexual favors were never an issue. I discovered early on that men like to dream, not act. When your business is money, sex takes a back seat. I had access to capital that was required for major real estate. I had the gold, so I could make the rules. At the International Council of Shopping Centers convention, a developer had one drink too many and flirted and pinched the derriere of an attractive woman at the cocktail reception. The woman turned out to be the wife of the senior mortgage lender of the John Hancock Life Insurance Company. That pinch cost him a $42 million loan! I witnessed that pinch and heard about the loan rejection a few days later. People could say whatever they wanted about me, but I was not an unattractive woman; I was just untouchable.

When traveling, torn between feeling a little lonely and a little out of place, I tried to take control of the situation—go into a casual restaurant at the hotel…find a man traveling by himself. Women didn't travel alone. Particularly in the south, I would be the only unattached woman at a restaurant. I would walk up to a distinguished looking man sitting alone. "Hey listen, I'm traveling on business. Would you like some companionship? I would appreciate just having someone to talk to." We would talk about family, his wife. It was better than sitting alone. I never had a pass made at me. Sometimes on planes, fellow business men would complain about their wives because they knew they would never see me again. I heard a lot of personal stories.

I also had to be careful with how the wives perceived me. One of my business associates would never tell his wife that I was going on the same business trip. It took years for the wives to realize I was a mother with two kids who went to the same schools and had the same problems.

My mother never discussed my job. She was a bright woman, but she would have preferred I stay home with my children rather than waste my time working. To my parents, I didn't have a career, but a job that was supporting my family. To say your daughter was divorced and living in New York with two children did not make them proud.

I'll never forget how my father responded when he was trying to decide if he should sell his company. I arranged a dinner with Jack Sonnenblick so that he could advise him. After my father explained his needs, Jack told him I was the right one to run his company if he should decide not to sell it. My father was incredulous. "What does she know about women's shoes? She couldn't know much." And that was the end of it. My father brushed me off. He had no comprehension of the responsibilities I had at work. Jack, a brilliant man and still a friend of mine, couldn't get over the fact that my father wouldn't even consider me to run his company. Eventually, my father had a stroke and I negotiated the sale for him. For the next 24 years, he couldn't speak, and I ended up handling all his affairs anyway.

As part of the first generation of women executives entering a man's profession, I was always charting unknown territory. Sometimes, being first made it easier for me than for women who followed in my footsteps. Men in later decades felt threatened as the second generation of women tried to step into their shoes. Anger developed towards the opposite sex and that anger frequently carried over into personal lives. In this regard, the second wave of women had a tougher time than we pioneers did. We didn't have that *natural wall* to confront. I find it difficult talking with them sometimes because they are so angry. These are close friends of mine, professional women, some married, all well known. They don't like men as I do. Sadly, they don't trust men either.

Unknowingly, I was a crusader for the next generation, creating my own standards in the workplace. However, these standards would not have been acceptable to feminists Gloria Steinem and Betty Friedan.

There was no history to examine that might have assisted me in making choices, no first hand reports of others who had been through it. Yet, in the end, history may confirm that perhaps I handled the pressures that developed in the most appropriate fashion.

"I am an 88-year-old retired school teacher, and as I look back over these years I am convinced that life can be very interesting and profitable to each individual. I would suggest that each person realize that God has a plan, a place and a purpose for each of us. You are not an accident; you are special. Remember you have talent and abilities that are waiting to be used."

—Ozema Kelley
Retired educator and Sunday school teacher, Alabama

SHIRLEY R. MARTZ

Shirley Martz was the first woman CPA, certified public accountant, to practice in the state of North Dakota, passing the CPA exam in 1946. Her career spanned 50 years in an all male world of commerce, culminating with the North Dakota CPA's Public Service Award.

Quite active in civic affairs, including boards, clubs, associations, and councils, along with raising five children, Shirley represented a modern woman who "had it all."

The Way I See It...

You always use what attributes you have. I took advantage of whatever I had, but I was also good at what I did.

The Red Headed CPA

My mother was a trailblazer in the 1930s in a small town in North Dakota. My parents owned a bank and when the Depression hit, they couldn't keep the bank operating without outside income. My dad found work as a bank collector in a city 200 miles away. He moved out, but he tried to come home every two weeks. My mother ran the bank during his absence—and my entire childhood. When other banks were closing, my crackerjack mother kept hers running. She even won awards from the North Dakota Bankers Association. I certainly learned from her and can probably attribute my entrepreneurial bug to her.

I majored in drama my first year of college, but I needed another challenge. I only took up accounting because it was the first thing in the catalog starting with "A." My friends said it was a good place for me because they thought I was smart, and "dumb people didn't go into that field." I graduated with honors and was elected to the honor society for business graduates.

When I started in public accounting practice, I was 24 years old, red-headed and not too ugly. While that might seem a plus, it was a mixed blessing in 1945. Around 100 women CPAs worked throughout the country, but in my state, there was only me. It was a man's arena and people were shocked to see me. Some of them wouldn't talk to me at all. The profession was quite chauvinistic, but that didn't hold me back. I learned to deal with discrimination—they either accepted me or not.

I was employed by an accounting firm when I succumbed to the charms of fellow CPA Baldwin Martz and we married in 1946. I took an instructor position at the University of North Dakota because that allowed us to live in student housing, the first housing available after the World War II shortage.

In 1948, Baldy and I were invited to become partners in a firm I had worked for in Minot, North Dakota. Being partners with your spouse was a bit unusual, but we managed quite well.

One year, we decided to accept an invitation to attend neighboring Minnesota's Society of CPAs' professional seminar in Minneapolis. Our separate registrations and accompanying fees were sent in and after traveling some 500 miles, we presented ourselves at the opening cocktail party. Unfortunately for me, this social was scheduled at the Minneapolis Athletic Club.

When we reached the reception desk, the young lady presiding looked at me disdainfully and inquired, "What are you doing here? This is for CPAs only." After some discussion, it was revealed that the party was scheduled for a male only bar and nothing on heaven or earth was going to allow me to invade those sacred premises. And in any event, "Who ever heard of a woman CPA?" My youthful feminine reaction was to cry.

My husband's was to raise the roof. I was allowed to sit in the reception room with a cocktail, and the visiting officials from the American Institute of Certified Public Accountants, AICPA, took turns leaving the party and coming out to visit with me. They allowed me to attend the next day's professional sessions. I didn't receive any refund of my registration fees and no apology from the host CPA Society.

We had a business partner with us for seven years. We were located in the boonies and had difficulty finding qualified employees to help with accounting. Our partner called me into his office and suggested that if I would step down from the partnership to "employee" status, it would be easier for us to hire help in the office. Young men didn't want to work for a woman. He was probably right, but I was insulted anyway. I didn't do it and we split up our partnership shortly after that.

Another time, my husband was trying to work with a difficult client. He thought a different perspective might help the situation. He informed the client I would be taking over. The client objected because I was a woman, and my husband reassured them. "She knows everything I know...she would be just as good for you." They still didn't take me.

I was quite an attractive woman, so many of our clients' wives hated me. After they met me, they didn't want their husbands to work with me. That sounds funny now, but it was not humorous then. I lost clients. Even after their husbands died, wives found it difficult to let me help them run their businesses. It took them a long time to like me and respect what I could do for them and their companies. If only they had known...my relationship with their husbands was the farthest thing from romantic. In the end, I knew everything about their corporations, so for their own welfare, they had to stay with me.

Maybe the time I spent with clients *was* intimate. People talk to their lawyers and doctors, and they talk to their accountants because they know it isn't going any further. They reveal secrets they wouldn't otherwise. I had a blue collar client who inherited his aunt's money. He came in on Secretary's Day and he saw flowers on the secretary's desk and he asked me why I didn't have any flowers. I told him, "I'm not a secretary and I guess accountants are not as important as secretaries."

Later that day, I received a bouquet of red roses as big as a football field, at least a $50 bouquet. I thought, "I *have* to thank him." He lived out of town and didn't have an office...he was a truck driver. If I wrote him a note, his wife would think, "What in the hell are you doing, sending flowers to this woman?" But I *had* to thank him, so I finally sent him a very formal note. I guess I was wrong. He never came in again. It must not have turned out very well for him after I sent the note.

I wasn't the least bit interested in anybody else's husband. I had five children, but they didn't know that. My husband was movie star handsome, but *he* never suffered any sex discrimination from his appearance.

Even though my looks sometimes created problems, I believe that you should use what attributes you have. I dealt with the IRS on a case basis all the time, and I usually fared well with them—partly because I was unusually attractive. The IRS agents were always men and my looks never seemed to be a problem with them. I took advantage of the situation. Why wouldn't I? I took advantage of whatever I could, but I was also good at what I did. You bet I was.

I didn't think about paving the way for the next generation of women; I wasn't concerned. I worked 70 hours a week at times, so I didn't have much free time. I was on the symphony board, the hospital board and the bank board. I was vice president of the state chamber of commerce and also the first president of the Quota Club, an organization similar to Kiwanis, but for women. No opportunity existed to join a man's club. Because they didn't have to take women, they didn't ask.

In 1988, the AICPA sent Baldy a certificate for 40 years of membership, along with a waiver for any future dues and a nice story in the local paper. We had both joined the organization at the same time in 1948. After waiting six months for similar recognition, I wrote them asking why my 40 years membership wasn't as worthy as his. I was sent an apology, the same waiver and certificate and an offer to send the very late story to the paper. I declined. I never received an explanation.

Looking back, I wouldn't do anything differently. We worked extremely hard and it was a mighty challenge. I met some interesting people along the way, too. At times, I would have liked to be home more with my children, but you can't have it all—you have to make choices. I would probably do the same thing again. I can't say I harbor regrets.

And I'm still a red head. I'll die a red head. It's all right.

Manufacturing

LORETTA KAMINSKY

Loretta Kaminsky is a breast cancer survivor. She attributes her cancer as the catalyst for starting her own business at 48-years-old. Lou-Retta's Custom Chocolates opened in 1983 and was featured on the front page of the USA Today *money section for Valentine's Day. The phone didn't stop ringing for Loretta until she sold her business 24 years later. Entrepreneurial by nature, she wanted to mold chocolate into something other than a square or a rectangle, so she created the "chocolate rose."*

She was named Small Business Advocate of the Year in New York State, elected Chair of the New York State Small Business Development Center Advisory Board, appointed to the National Advisory Board of Women's Business Research Network, appointed to the Governor's New York State Small Business Advisory Board, won the Vanguard Award for Women Owned Business, and won the Governor's Award for Excellence in Business.

Guest appearances included Salle Jesse Raphael *and* Good Day New York. *Her products appeared on the* Today Show, Live with Regis and Kathy Lee *and* CBS This Morning. *Her clients included Walt Disney World, Porcshe, Domino Pizza, QVC, Saks, and the L.A. Raiders.*

The Way I See It...

When you are dealing in a male-oriented world, you don't have to be a door mat or a barracuda. If you can hit that middle ground, you will find success.

The Chocolate Rose

In 1973, I was diagnosed with breast cancer and had a double mastectomy. I was 37 years old. Up to that time, I was a happy housewife and mother of three children. I had a great life as a kindergarten teacher. But with cancer, my whole life changed. I decided to find a way to leave my mark on the world so people would know I had been here. It became very important for me—a burning desire—so I started a business.

My girlfriends thought I was absolutely insane. None of them worked. They couldn't understand why I wanted to start a company. "Your husband is highly successful...you don't need to work...you have a great life." I *did* have a great life. But when something happens like breast cancer and you don't know if you're going to survive, you start thinking about what you have accomplished.

I was an excellent baker, mainly because my husband loved sweets. My friends started asking if I would sell my desserts. It didn't take long for the idea to dawn on me that I could sell to other people too. Settling on a clever name, *Desserts by Loretta* was born, and I started baking desserts in my kitchen.

My children were growing up and leaving for college. When they came home for the holidays, they weren't too happy that I was busy with my business instead of busy with them, giving them my undivided attention.

Customers started asking if I could make chocolate. I found a place to teach me and thought, "Maybe this is what I was meant to do!" I met with a molds maker. I had an idea to make a chocolate rose. "I want to do chocolate in dimension; have you ever done it?"

He thought about it and said, "No, but it sounds interesting, so let's do it."

My chocolate shop was born.

The first obstacle was, of course, going to a bank. This was 1984 and women were not exactly burning up the bushes in business. The banker took one look at me and said, "This enterprise sounds like a nice little idea. Now go home and get your husband and bring him back to sign for the loan." It was totally disheartening because I knew I could run this business on my own. Without a choice, I had to ask my husband to sign for my first loan.

My second challenge was how to sell these wonderful three dimensional roses, vases and candy boxes. I started calling all the major businesses in Buffalo. I was a 48-year-old woman whose husband was an extremely successful attorney. They politely made appointments with me. Invariably, each time I met with a prospective client, the conversation was the same. "At this stage of your life, why are you doing this?"

I answered honestly. "To make a great deal of money. Why are you doing what you're doing?"

Well, that shut them up! If I had been a man meeting with them about a business deal, that piece of conversation would never have happened.

Little by little, I started selling to major companies. Then I had a brilliant idea. I called my local newspaper to do a story about me. I actually wanted to be in *USA Today*, but I knew I needed the local story to send to the money section editor of *USA Today*. I needed credibility. About three months later, I received a call from a *USA Today* reporter. After a ninety minute interview, he asked, "How would you like to be the feature in the money section on Valentine's Day?"

I had an 1,100 square foot facility where I made chocolate in the back and sold it in the front. As soon as the article came out, my phone started ringing off the hook. No one knew I was just this little candy maker in Buffalo. The first call was Lancome Cosmetics. They wanted me to duplicate their lipstick in chocolate. I didn't know how I was going to do it, but I said, "Of course." I went back to the mold maker and did 80,000 of them.

A man in the Japan Travel Bureau presented me with my next challenge. He wanted to come to Buffalo and meet with me. I called my friend at the World Trade Center, asking for advice. She helped me understand the cultural implications of this business deal. "There aren't too many women entrepreneurs in Japan now, so I suggest bringing your husband to the meeting. I think the Japanese representative would be much more comfortable with a man present." I asked my husband to join me as an *observer*. This was my job and my business, after all. He agreed. In the meantime, I had asked my banker for a credit check on the Japan Travel Bureau. She shared with me what she had discovered. "Wow, they did $8 million in sales and they are the largest travel agency in Japan—don't show them your books!"

We met with Mr. Hatanaka. I would tell him what my company could do and he would respond to my husband who would respond to me. We had a circle of communication going. We had lunch at a lovely restaurant when my husband turned to Mr. Hatanaka. "Did you know my wife has a black belt in shopping?" There went my credibility. I was trying to be this professional business woman, and my husband was making jokes about me. Mr. Hatanaka laughed. He thought it was quite charming. I almost killed my husband.

Two weeks later, we met with Mr. Hatanaka and all the principals of the Japan Travel Bureau at their gorgeous palatial offices on 5th Avenue in New York. My husband, my company's attorney, accompanied me because we had to sign contracts. Mr. Hatanaka turned to the CEO of his company and said, "By the way, did you know Mrs. Kaminsky has a black belt in shopping?" It became a standing joke. It was one of the many times in my life that I realized being a woman entrepreneur had extra obstacles to overcome. Even though it broke the ice, I was sure that it stayed with them. I was an extremely accomplished business woman and did a fabulous project for them, maybe 200,000 boxes of chocolates, but I am sure that was the one thing that stuck in their mind. Every time I came to New York, they would tell me who was having a sale.

Without my husband, I don't think I could have consummated the deal. I never did anything one on one with the Japanese. It didn't hurt my feelings because whatever it took, I would do. I read quite a few books on Japanese protocol. In the end, I got the deal done.

I sold my business 24 years later to a male-owned company because I was the leader in the industry. It was gratifying to me that I had persevered being a woman.

My husband, who attended many business meetings with me, shared an observation that holds true for all women in business: "If you can learn to walk the fine line between a door mat and a barracuda, you will become successful at anything you endeavor." It's the truth.

I was fortunate that I had a knack for relationship building. When I walked into a contract and met an ice wall, I would show them what I could do and why they should choose my company. Saks, Disney, Home Shopping Network, it didn't matter. I had to go one step further to prove I was better than the others. The obstacle became a challenge—something I couldn't wait to do instead of something I didn't want to do—the ultimate challenge! Twenty-five years ago, women were intimidated. If they were rebuffed, many wouldn't try again. I *knew* I could do the job.

It took seven years before the bank put my business loan into my name. It upset me. Every year, I would ask and they would say your credit is great and we are reviewing your loan. Finally, I stormed in and went directly to the loan officer. "Enough! I have a track record—you can see what I am doing. I want this loan out of my husband's name."

I've worked hard over the years to see that progressive changes have been made for women in the workplace. I had no idea I was going to accomplish the things I did in my business. Some incredible things have happened to me. I have served on national boards and met outstanding women. It goes to prove we have things inside us we don't know are there.

I became successful and very high profile. My husband supported me every step of the way. He once said to me, "You are a much more interesting person now than you ever were before."

Technology

P.S. "TERRI" CARR

Six days after college, at age 21, Terri Carr went to work for IBM and stayed 30 years. IBM grew quickly, and in 1966, when Terri graduated, the company was desperate for men or women armed with science or math degrees. Luckily, Terri had one. A quintessential career woman, she served all across the United States in a myriad of management positions, acquiring status as IBM's "model woman manager." Not once did she ever report to another woman.

Along her career path, she became one of the first women in business to become actively involved in several Junior Leagues around the country, paving the way for others to follow.

Upon retiring with her second husband to their dream house in Sun Valley, Idaho, her husband died, and her second career began with an international software company. After five years of global marketing, she decided it was time to retire.

Today, as a community volunteer, Terri is heavily involved with the Orange County, California chapter of SCORE, Service Corps of Retired Executives; ARCS, Achievement Rewards for College Scientists; the Volunteer Center; and, of course, the Junior League.

The Way I See It...

I knew I had to do *whatever I had to do* to get ahead. I never thought about being a man or a woman. I just needed to compete.

One of IBM's Firsts

Women were supposed to go into teaching...or teaching...or teaching. Not me. I wanted a math degree.

My mother panicked. "What are you going to do with it?"

I tried to reassure her. "Something will come up."

Six days after I graduated from college in 1966, I landed a job at IBM. I had just turned 21. Lucky for me, the company had announced a new computer for sale and they needed a full staff of people with scientific backgrounds to install them. I had a math degree and that was good enough for IBM.

Everyone was impressed, but no one understood what I was going to be. "What is a systems engineer?"

In my training class, I met people who had graduate degrees from Yale or Harvard. My degree was from the University of New Mexico. I was so naïve. Nevertheless, my parents raised me to think that I could do anything. I knew I had to do *whatever I had to do* to get ahead. Being a woman didn't enter my mind. I just needed to compete.

Once I started my new position, I wrote computer programs that ran the businesses for IBM's clients. At my age, the responsibility was enormous, but I didn't think it strange. One of my clients said to me years later, "I couldn't believe I had a 23-year-old woman running my business." IBM couldn't replace me with a man, because only a few people even understood what I was doing.

I never thought I would be working beyond three years. I was told that IBM would recoup the cost of training their employees in three years. After working one year, I married and thought, "I've done one year and have two to go...I'll quit and have babies." But I enjoyed my work and decided to wait to have children. It never occurred to me that I would achieve recognition for being with IBM for 25 years!

I was one among a company of competitive men. We all wanted to get ahead, but the men had a major advantage that I didn't. They could ride dirt bikes, play basketball or go out drinking with the boss. As the one and only woman in the company, no one wanted me tagging along. The social aspect was half of getting ahead on the job.

Some customers were uncomfortable with a woman as a manager, but since only a few people could do my job, they had no choice. My early years were spent managing different accounts: gravel producer, lumber operator, Indian jewelry manufacturer, a bank, a dairy. I was used any place. When I was on-site, I loved learning about the different professions. In one small New Mexico town, I was writing all the programs for a mining company. I kept asking, "When can I see the mine?"

After four months, they finally gave me an answer "We will never take you down there because it's bad luck to have a woman in the mine." End of discussion.

Being a woman often created problems. When I met a fellow office employee in the ticket line at the Southwest Airlines counter, we started chatting. The clerk noticed how friendly we were. "Oh, since you two know each other, you could get a love fare." The promotion would have saved half the airfare, but explaining the shared ticket to the expense department was out of the question. They would never have believed it.

Because so few women traveled for business in the early 1970s, we were easily recognized. As I boarded an airplane, a stewardess I had never met looked at me intently. "You cut your hair!" She saw so few women on a continuing basis that she remembered me.

I went to dine alone at Brennan's restaurant in New Orleans and was told by the owner to come back tomorrow with a reservation. Hoping he would change his mind, I said, "I have to work."

He was shocked. "You work? Come on, I will seat you now."

IBM presented a very competitive work environment for me. I never worked for a woman my entire career and few women were at my level. As a female manager in 1976, I attended class after class as IBM's spokesperson and model manager. Several programs were eventually adopted to encourage more female managers. Being a spokesperson did not endear me with the male managers though. My absence meant that one of them would have to do my job.

For three years, I was a User Group Manager in Atlanta, responsible for interfacing with about 14,000 customers. Only three such managers existed in the country and, more than likely, I was the first female. I met my future husband and moved to California where I had a series of positions. I created the business partners program in Orange County and was even the project manager for the tallest building there. Once you are hired as a manager at IBM, they expect you to be able to manage anything.

My career path was a bit odd. I had a foot in two cultures at the same time: I was a professional person and a volunteer in the non-profit organization, Junior League. The year I joined the League, I was the only provisional professional to join. Most people didn't do both. They wouldn't even try. Other Junior Leaguers were surprised to hear that I worked. I remember attending a training meeting with my flat calendar in front of me so I could make sure that I had recorded all the dates for my appointments. Another volunteer sitting next to me leaned over. "You're going to be in Dallas, then New York and then here and then there?" She didn't know what to make of me. I was gone all the time.

My career transfers resulted in my serving with five different Junior Leagues across the country. Each year, more professional women were on the League board. When I joined my last one in Orange County, California, they started doing night meetings for the general population. I was a member of the first board that had a night meeting. Now, all the meetings are at night because everybody is a professional.

The Junior League was something I needed to do. It was a group of women and I was around men all the time. In the Dallas League in the '70s, I helped a couple of women with career training. They both could have bought and sold Dallas, but they wanted to go to work. I found this interesting; I was going crazy at work with an exhausting job, wishing I could take a break, and they had children to raise and still wanted to go into the work place.

Most of the career women I knew were not married and did not have children. Women were getting bombarded by the press on this issue during my early career. I recall a national study that said if a woman was not married by a certain age, she had a better chance of getting hit by lightning than of getting married. As a result, some women succumbed to the pressure and tried to have both a career and a family life. Of course, no one around me did it.

Nearing retirement from IBM, my second husband and I built a house in Sun Valley, Idaho and before we could move, he died. So, on a sad note, I started my second career with a software company that interfaced with IBM. I managed a global marketing program for them, traveling to Europe as well as the States. After that, I started to think I'd had enough and needed to stay home. I had worked 35 years. I started so young and now it was time to rest.

When I began my career, IBM was looking for people to do a job and I did it successfully. If I had not been successful, they would not have promoted me or moved me to other positions. Sometimes I would work all night. I faced many struggles and challenges. I personally advanced the status of women across the nation. Many times, I was the first woman and sometimes the first *person* to do a job and do it well. I dealt with a commuting marriage, not exactly in vogue at the time and other personal situations that had to be managed and I still did the job.

I believe you have to be passionate about what you want to do. Study hard. Work hard. Don't underestimate how hard you'll have to work and how much you'll have to give. I learned that networking was a key component, in and out of the company. It did not occur to me to do anything differently because I was a woman. It never entered my mind. If I had to do it over, I would not change a thing.

Interior Design

POTA VURNAKES VALLAS

Born in 1910, Pota Vallas has lived in Raleigh, North Carolina for 85 years. She still lives in the same house her husband built for her 59 years ago. She came to America from Sparta, Greece at the age of 14, evolving over the years into the beloved matriarch of the city's Greek community.

She pursued a dream of owning her own company, an interior design studio. The first company owned by a Greek woman in the state, National Art Interiors opened in 1944 and grew into a $5 million company. After working well into her nineties, Pota decided to retire and sell her company.

Giving back to her community was important to her. Instrumental in the building of her church, Holy Trinity Greek Orthodox Church, she donated three acres of land for its construction…and, in recognition of her value to First Citizens Bank, she was named to their board of directors in 1986.

The Way I See It...

My friends thought a woman's place was at home, cooking and raising her children, but I thought a woman could serve a greater purpose.

With All Her Heart

When I came to the United States, I felt so *little*...I was ashamed to go to school and afraid to go to someone's home. I was very shy. But I found courage. I believe women should have courage, with a capital C.

I lived as a child in one of the oldest villages in Sparta, Greece, thousands of years old. As an intern at a small polytechnic school, I was introduced to the field of design. My dream to pursue this field would begin there and travel with me to the United States.

My father loved everything about America and wanted to bring his family to Raleigh, North Carolina. He came over to America first to establish our home. The rest of us would come later as he could afford our passage. He opened a fruit stand and soda fountain and will always be remembered as the city's first Greek immigrant.

In 1924, he came to Greece and brought me back with him to Raleigh. I was 14 years old. When the stock market crashed in 1929, he lost our home and the business. He had just enough money to start another business—a candy, ice cream and sandwich store. It took until 1939 to bring my mother and sisters over, just as Nazi Germany was about to invade Greece.

In the early 1940s, it was very questionable for a woman to work. My friends thought a woman's place was at home, cooking and raising her children, but I thought a woman could serve a greater purpose. I knew I could run my household *and* work.

My husband was in the restaurant business, but I could not bear to think of my daughters working there. Restaurants were different then. Horrible, unsavory clientele came to the restaurant...waitresses cursed and slept with soldiers. I didn't want my children to know them. I wanted to shield them from that element. This helped fuel my desire to start my own business.

I applied for a job at the Singer Sewing Company and taught sewing lessons on the side. I began to see a different class of people—kind people with good hearts who wanted nice things in their houses. It felt good to help them. I made the decision right then and there that these were the type of people I wanted my children to be around.

Working for Singer, demonstrating sewing machines at the State Fairgrounds was tough. I worked like a dog, day and night, every day of the week, 12 hours a day. I didn't want them to think a little foreign girl could let them down.

When my boss was killed in an automobile accident, the home office decided to make me the temporary manager. The ten salesmen would not accept me as their boss because I was a woman. They accepted me as an employee but not as a manager. The two women bookkeepers didn't like me because I was Greek. I hung on for four years until the company wanted to move me to Richmond, ironically, for a man's job. I didn't go. I had made up my mind: it was time to start my own business.

In 1944, my husband George and I went to New York so I could take a course in interior design. We stayed at the Hotel St. George on 42nd Street. I went to school at night and worked without pay for a Jewish designer during the day. He taught me everything he knew. When I left for Raleigh, he agreed to send me fabric and George paid him $10,000. George then bought me a building in Raleigh for my new business and National Art Interiors, my dream, was finally a reality.

George financed my business as much as possible, but there came a time when I had to go to a bank. First Citizens Bank took over my financing and I pulled my way out of debt into prosperity and profit. The bank was one of my first major customers—I decorated 103 bank branches. Eventually, I was named to the board.

In the early days of my career, people thought a woman should not be exposed to the outside world, for fear the world would be brought into their homes. I knew I had a talent and it *had* to come out. Many people told me that I needed to try. Some doubted me when I told them I was going into business in 1944. They said I wouldn't succeed; it wasn't the right time to grow a business. Statements like this depressed me to the last degree, but I did what I thought was the best thing for Pota Vallas. The American people backed me up after they saw how I conducted the business. Eventually, the people in my church and many who doubted me came to my store and accepted me.

Over the years, I noticed that men would take advantage of women. I knew women had so much talent, but they were still put down by men. A woman is smarter than a man in many cases. A woman can do three things at the same time. She can take care of her home, take care of her children and take care of her work. I don't believe a man can do that. Men come home and play with their children, but they don't know how to make a family. The biggest column in a household is the woman. The woman is the column of the *world*.

In many ways, women are stronger than men because they have been discriminated against by men. I always rose above all the people who would try to put me down. I paid no attention to any discrimination towards me because I was a woman. I was a role model for others to follow, starting with my own children. I showed women that it is possible to follow your dream. It was not easy; I had many sleepless nights and shed many tears. I also had the greatest husband a woman could have. And every night, I asked the help of the Lord, and with Him, I achieved success.

If I had to live my life over, I would not change a thing.

Education

DR. BETTY L. SIEGEL

Betty Siegel was the first woman academic dean at two different universities; the first woman to lead an institution in the university system of Georgia; and the longest serving woman president of a public university in the country. President of Kennesaw State for 25 years, she took an enrollment of 4,000 students to over 18,000 when she retired.

Georgia Governors Zell Miller and Sonny Perdue appointed her to serve on several commissions, and during the city of Atlanta's Olympic year, she chaired the Board of Directors of the Chamber of Commerce. She was the first woman to hold this position. Corporate board seats include Atlanta Gas & Light, Equifax and NSI, as well as community boards, Arby's Foundation, Atlanta Ballet, Boy Scouts of Atlanta and the CDC Foundation Advisory Board.

Among her many awards are the Georgia Woman of the Year; 100 Most Influential Georgians; Women in Business Lifetime Achievement Award; Cobb County Citizen of the Year; 20 Women Making a Mark on Atlanta; Howard Washington Thurman Ecumenical Award; and the first-ever Lifetime Achievement Award from the YWCA of NW Georgia.

She holds the Betty L. Siegel Endowed Chair of Leadership, Ethics and Character at Kennesaw and was awarded six honorary doctorates from other universities.

Betty played a major role in the advancement of women's positions in the field of education. Today, she continues her leadership development agenda as an internationally known lecturer and motivational speaker.

The Way I See It...

I think it is harder for women to have it all. Men have a better support group than women do. It is critical that women know what they can and cannot do.

A Coal Miner's Daughter

I grew up in the 1930s in a mountain community of four generations. I'm an Appalachian and I *claim* it. I have never been ashamed of my heritage. "Poor little coal miner's kids" are not what people think they are. They are tenacious in spirit and healthy in mind...never sorry or fearful. When meeting someone, my grandmother would say a most marvelous thing. "Who are his people?" When complimenting someone, she would say, "They are not sorry people." She meant that our people are not apologetic. They have dignity. The "people" legacy in the mountains is strong.

I was expected to live out the promise of smart...to be a credit to the family. My mother never asked me or my sister to do chores around the house. We were to study...always to study. I was a smart girl, an apt learner, and eventually became valedictorian of my class. At 16 years of age, as president of a youth roundtable in Kentucky, I was invited to go to the White House to meet President Truman. I still remember going to Knoxville to buy a new coat to wear to the White House. It meant the world to me.

I was supposed to do anything a man could do. My father taught me to be a tomboy, to ride horses and play football. I didn't think in terms of a man having it "better." In fact, women had it better. Women were teachers, community leaders and business owners... matriarchs who kept faith and families together. When my father came to own the mine he worked in, my mother decided to be president of the company. My father's mother, unable to read or write, ended up owning the largest boarding house in the area during the Depression.

My path was taught to me. I used the same qualities I learned from those wonderful women and put them to work. I was just one of a whole army of women who did significant work and did it with grace…and with all kinds of hardships, I'm sure.

Everybody has hardships, moments of disappointment and extraordinary failures. But the important part is your reaction to it and your attitude toward it. We are bound by our own limitations.

I never thought I would be president of a college, ever. It's very humbling and amazing to me.

After high school, I went away to a little mountain college, Cumberland. Then on to Wake Forest University, the University of North Carolina at Chapel Hill and Florida State University. My areas of study were child psychology and administration.

At Cumberland College, I made one foray into the medical field when I briefly considered becoming a doctor. It was the only instance in my life when I was not perceived as a star. The experience proved to be a critical turning point for me. Coming from a very poor mountain high school, I entered the required chemistry class with no background in the subject. I was the only female in a class of men. After the professor asked me some questions, I was so embarrassed, I dropped the class. I have always been uncomfortable when I am not smart enough in a situation. I assumed I didn't have a place in the medical profession. Perhaps it might have been different if the professor had encouraged me.

Of course, women professors were scarce. I never had a woman professor at Wake Forest or Chapel Hill. All my role models in education were men.

When I began my professional career in the 1960s, administration was still not a place for women. Few women principals existed and exceedingly fewer superintendents. I came to the University of Florida as the first woman professor in a large prestigious department of men. I showed up six months pregnant. They had never had a woman professor and, to my knowledge, definitely not a pregnant woman professor. My doctor advised me. "Don't tell them you're pregnant…just go down there and show up." When I arrived in September, I was told by a faculty member that pregnant women have no place in this university. But nobody made me leave.

I decided to have some fun by announcing that I was going to have my baby at quarter break and never miss a class. Lo and behold, I had the baby on the quarter break, didn't miss a day and came back in January!

Being the first woman is never easy for anyone. A groundbreaker has no sure knowledge of what is expected. And you surely don't know what others say when you are not around.

Typically, the university had a steak supper for all the men when they hired a new professor. When they hired the next *woman* professor, my friend and I dressed up in my husband's clothes and took a cigar along and acted like we were men. It absolutely broke them up in stitches. No woman had ever gone to one of their parties, much less dominated it. That's chutzpah. It could have been devastating, but they didn't let that happen. To this day, it's a legendary story in that department—"remember when our two women professors dressed up like men to remind us they were women?"

Two years after that, I won the best teacher award. Then, administration started looking for a dean. There had never been a woman academic dean in the state of Florida. My name was put forth with about 100 applicants and I was offered the job. I turned it down at first—not interested. Mary McCauley, my friend and author of the *Meyers Briggs Test*, was with me the day I was offered the job. We were at a conference called *Women Breaking into Management* and we were sitting together. I told her I wasn't going to take the job, and she very pointedly told me I had to take it. In the end, I did.

In one of the articles written about me when I accepted the dean's job, the reporter described me as if I were in a fashion show: "Dr. Betty Siegel, dressed in a red suit and beige blouse, looking like a model, will be the dean of..." Instead of describing my skill set, they zeroed in on what I was wearing. In the same article, another dean was also described, but not for his stylish attire.

A large black tie dinner was given in our honor. Everyone thought my husband was the new dean because he was in the receiving line with me. I saw and heard non-verbal and verbal expressions from people who were surprised that a woman would be in that role.

Naturally, I became interested in women's roles and became the spokesperson for women in Florida, developing women's programs and a women's center.

When I came to my own college, Kennesaw, no women administrators had been hired. We developed leadership centers for women, joined boards and sought out professional places of prominence. Every woman owes it to another woman. I always like to say "if you see a turtle on a post, it didn't get there by itself." I was invited to dozens of associations that never featured women speakers: Rotary, Kiwanis and many others. I did that by design —I would not turn down a speech anywhere. I belonged to almost every woman's group in the country.

Women had no role models. All the books slanted towards men and their way of leadership. I read everything. Books similar to *Dress for Success* came out advising women to power dress—how you've got to put on your safari helmet and jacket and wrestle all the animals in the jungle to their knees. I searched for role models. Women's rights author and advocate Betty Friedan became instrumental in my life. Gloria Steinem was in my generation. My truest hero in the world is Frances Hesselbein of the Girl Scouts and Drucker Foundation. She paved the way for me to see myself as a leader. I became absorbed with leadership. I met Ken Blanchard and shared his beliefs...that it wasn't just your gender that mattered.

I once interviewed for another university president's job and the search committee didn't realize that one of my friends served on their committee. After the process, my friend told me what the chairman of the committee said about my interview. "If that had been a man, we would have hired her on the spot." I didn't make the cut on that job, but his statement tells you something about what that search committee was looking for.

Sitting in a dean's meeting once, someone kept saying, "The dean should do this because *he...* "

I said to him, "Don't you want to say he *or* she?"

He said, "Oh Betty, you're right, but I'm going to give you the highest compliment...I think you think like a man." I don't think like a man. I think like a human.

I have been the first woman on five corporate boards, several on the national level. I was privileged to be on those boards, and I was appointed to a few 25 years ago. I was part of them because they were aware they needed diversity. To be the first woman on a board was a wonderful affirmation, but, more than that, it was a responsibility.

As leaders, we must be thoughtful about why we are doing the things we are doing at each stage of our life.

One area I find most troubling in my life as a woman is how to do it all. It is very hard for women leaders who love being parents or love being a spouse. Every woman leader I know has said, "I wish I had a wife." It is harder for women…men have support and women do not. It is critical that women know what they cannot do. I must have $5,000 in unused salon massages. Everyone gives them to me and I don't use them. I can't get there. I have too much to do. I don't know how to allot time to myself and I suffer the consequences. I must have 750 cookbooks. I can't cook. I hate to cook. I hate to come home and start supper. But people know I collect cookbooks so they give them to me.

One of the things I would have done differently is exercise more and take more vacations. We have three homes…one is a mountain retreat that is pristine pure. We call it Wind Stowe, which means Place of Joy. I went up there *one* time last year. Women must learn in the future to do better than that.

I did the best I could at the time I did it. I was there for my family—my husband Joel and my two sons, David and Michael. At least, I hope they would say that.

Music

LOUISE HARRISON

Louise Harrison is the only sister of George Harrison, the beloved band member and guitarist of The Beatles, the band that redefined rock and roll. One would think Louise's life has been an easy ride, but this Liverpool native has had her share of ups and downs. Yet, she retains a remarkable sensitivity to others and life in general.

After her famous brother died, Louise set out to keep The Beatles alive...because as her father believed..."whatever you decide to do, just keep going and you will probably succeed."

The Way I See It...
We are on this earth to help each other and be kind. We are one after all.

Love, Love, Love
When I was a little girl, I read a lot of fairy tales, and thought that I, too, would marry a prince and live happily ever after. But things don't work out that way.

I grew up in Liverpool and was still there when World War II broke out. I remember bombs dropping around us, killing many people each night. Unlike 9/11, when people were encouraged to live in fear, back in WW II-Britain, we looked at the Germans and said, "Hey, you think you're going to scare us? You show your face around here and we'll tear you limb from limb!" We definitely did not live in *fear*!

My mom and dad were fabulous parents…young and very much like kids at heart…always supportive, teaching us right from wrong.

Early on, I asked my dad what I had to do to be a good person and he said "never do anything to harm or upset other creatures on the planet." Such a simple way to put it, isn't it?

My mom and dad were Louise and Harold. I had three brothers. I am often asked if I have musical talents and I jokingly say, "No, I have no musical talents! My parents had four kids and I was the first and it wasn't until the fourth one that they got it right." That was George. My other two brothers were Harold James and Peter Henry.

One of the first things you had to learn growing up in Liverpool was how to make fun of yourself, because if you didn't, everyone else would. You also learned never to take yourself too seriously…you took your tasks in life seriously, but never yourself. Even if you achieved something good, you didn't go bragging about it. It wasn't the proper thing to do.

Music was always playing in the house through a radio that our uncle had made. My dad had a beautiful soprano voice and had been a singer in the church choir when they were starting to build the cathedral in Liverpool. He also learned to play the guitar when I was very small. We just all loved music. When George, John and Paul started playing together, my mom was probably the only one of the parents who would tolerate all of that noise. They would practice in the upstairs bedroom.

The boys met in their teens. John had started a band at his high school called the Quarry Men. Paul and George went to the same school in downtown Liverpool, and they met on the bus and became friends. My parents were very supportive of the boys when they started getting fan letters from all over the world. Their first reaction was, "Okay, we'll answer them." More than 1,000 letters a day arrived! They would go through them and try to answer every one of them with a hand written note.

Lately much has been said in the news about Martin Scorsese, the film director, and his plans to do a documentary about George and his spirituality. As far as I know, he hasn't talked to anybody that knew George before he was a Beatle. George's spirituality started long before he ever met Ravi Shankar, sitar virtuoso, or Maharishi, founder of Transcendental Meditation. Actually the way our parents brought us up wasn't really religious; it was more spiritual.

I was sent to a Catholic school with a nun headmistress who, in her own way, was fond of me. She was strict and didn't know how to show love. All the nuns offered me the same advice on a successful life. "Do as you are told, get down on your knees and pray. And if you are good enough, you might become a nun." That was their whole scope on life. But our parents looked at life differently and taught us that the Creator is how you get your good ideas. That's why we call it the Creator! You don't have to go anywhere to find God. Just look inside yourself.

By the time George was a Beatle, that philosophy was already part of his subconscious. When he met people who believed differently from the Western idea of religion—that you must go to church wearing your best hat and let everybody see how holy you are, putting money in the plate, yet it's okay to be mean and nasty during the week as long as you go to church on Sunday—he rejected that whole idea. He found other religions across the world that believed the Creator was the spark of light within you. He was able to relate to the thought that spirituality came from within.

Unfortunately, whatever they put in this documentary won't necessarily be how George developed into a spiritual person. I have been asked how Martin Scorsese knows about George's spirituality. I don't know because he hasn't approached any of the members of George's biological-living family. I would guess that none of the people who have written books about The Beatles actually knew any of them from the time they were born.

People talk about the quest to find yourself, but we never had any quest to find ourselves. We always knew who we were. I'm Lou Harrison. My parents were Lou and Harold Harrison. I have three brothers and that's who I am. One of my goals is to never bring disgrace to that family...to be a credit in whatever way my potential leads me. Mom and Dad always said they would do their best to be honorable and decent people regardless of what fate had in store for them.

As I understand it...it is the Creator that *provides* our ideas and *we act* on them. If we don't, they are wasted. I don't like to use the word God because it is a connotation that the so-called "Religious Right" use. I call it either the Creator or the Supreme Being. I have my own name for it as well. I spell it Kozzmau. I envision one Star Trek episode where there is a huge chunk of vibrating light, a mass of intelligent energy. That's how I see the Creator. I cannot imagine any such powerful Force limiting itself to a human gender. Each living being has a drop of that.

After traveling to many countries in the Northern Hemisphere, I married an engineer and moved to the United States in 1963. The Beatles had a record contract by then and my mom started sending me copies of their records. My immediate response was to take discs to the radio stations, telling them about my kid brother's band from England. I studied *Cashbox*, *Billboard* and *Variety* magazines (there was no *Rolling Stone* then) and wrote to Brian Epstein, The Beatles manager, with advice on how to break into the United States. The Beatles were with a very minor record label and I advised him to get Columbia, Capital or RCA, one of the three major ones. I found out that DJ's wouldn't play their records unless they were known and backed with real money. I also suggested they needed to get on the *Ed Sullivan Show*.

One day, as Ed Sullivan was coming into the London airport and The Beatles were there with mobs of people, he decided to find out who handled those guys. Of course, Brian had his calls closely monitored due to the popularity of The Beatles, but because I had constantly told him about Ed Sullivan, he took the call and the rest is history.

After many months of approaching radio stations about my kid brother's band, I realized it would make me sound more *official* if I could just say I was the U.S rep for the group, but Brian said he had "important people" that would do that. At the same time, I was writing to George Martin and Dick James, record producers, and they told me I should keep asking Brian to be named a representative because there was nobody more gung-ho and enthusiastic than me.

After the guys did the *Ed Sullivan Show,* crazy reports sprung up everywhere on the radio. One story came from *The Beatles* attending a charity ball in Washington, D.C. at an Ambassador's home. One of the young guests cut a chunk out of Ringo's hair. He was furious. The radio report however, said it was the Ambassador's wife, and that she had wrestled Ringo to the floor. I knew this wasn't true because I was standing with her at the back of the room. I called the station and the manager asked me to come on the air and give the correct report. I was a little timid at that time, so I declined.

That same manager called me back three days later and asked me to write a 60-second Beatles report each day for broadcast. I had been reading fan letters and trying to answer them, so I talked to George about it. He promised me that he would call in and tell me what was going on each day with The Beatles so I could report it.

The radio station soon wanted ten 60-second reports a week and I was paid the union scale.

It took off. The response from the listeners was tremendous. When the spots were no longer on the air, everyone wanted to know where Louise was. The station got over 600 calls in a matter of hours! So we started up again and this time, he added more stations and I received $30 from each of them. I didn't understand money and business too well then, and I still don't. I wasn't doing it for the money, but for the fans. Also, it did humor my husband because I spent so much money on Beatle postage.

The reports were broadcast on 22 major AM stations for about 18 months. The radio stations might not have been number one in their town, but after they carried The Beatles reports, they became the number one.

In Minneapolis, the competition contacted me and offered me double the money to switch to them. When I told them I was doing it for the fans, not the money, they were a little bit annoyed. They reported me to the union because I wasn't a union member. They threatened to bring lawsuits against the other stations. But the fans believed in me. I did not intend to switch for the money. Where would my credibility be?

Even after all of these years, I'm still working today, just like then, to keep The Beatles' music, love and compassion alive.

In the nineties, I started a non-profit organization called Drop-In, which stood for Determined to Restore Our Planet. I realized our planet's environment was changing for the worse. I thought that if we united The Beatles fans for a worthy cause we could make a difference. The organization was established in 16 countries and formed for Beatles fans to come together. We called them DROPS. It was the notion that if we had enough DROPS, we would form a huge wave of change…and get people to begin thinking about the environment. Toward the end of the century, though, the joke was on me. My "non-profit" was non-profitable beyond my wildest dreams! I had to stop the organization. People didn't donate money.

Because I was George's sister, they assumed I already had millions of dollars…which, of course, was never the case. I just wanted to do something good with The Beatles Fans to help the earth.

Right after George died, I met Marty Scott, who was like George in so many ways. I immediately adopted him! I took a Kozzmau attitude: I believed that my brother's being felt I still needed a brother. Marty and I formed a brother-sister relationship. He wanted to start a band that looked and sounded like The Beatles. It wasn't just about the music to me. I wanted the kind of guys George would have enjoyed hanging out with as well as the music. The band was formed and they selected the name, *Liverpool Legend*. They perform at the Starlite Theatre in Branson, Missouri. Of course, Marty performs as George. Listening to them, I close my eyes and I hear *The Beatles*.

People say to me, "Your brother must be very proud." It is such a good band and people leave the theatre glowing. I feel privileged to be able to do something I enjoy, and has everyone going away happy from the theatre.

Whenever I am asked about being related to someone famous, I simply say that I learned to mind my own business unless there was a reason to get involved. I accidentally became involved with my brother's famous band for the right reasons *before* they had any fame or fortune, not for my own personal gain or glory. If someone you know or love becomes wildly famous, be happy for them and be sorry for them. They will need your support and love because their normal life will be turned upside down. Comfort them when they have some down time and treat them like they are still the person they were when you first met them, rather than the famous person that others only think they know.

Ringo Starr remembers visiting some of his relatives in Liverpool one day and they started treating him differently, wanting him to sit in their special chairs, not where he usually would sit. He just wanted things to be normal like before the fame.

It's hard being famous.

Of course, no one necessarily has more trouble than anyone else. It's all a matter of perspective. When a person goes through difficulties, the problems being faced are always major, regardless of the scale. The most important thing is to draw on your own strength and manifest it to the people around you—be helpful and encourage them.

I was able to see my brother, George, for about an hour or so before he died. It was an hour that I will always remember. George had tried to live his life as the Great Spirit would want him to live. In the end he wasn't George Harrison of *The Beatles*, he was my brother.

I now live in Branson, Missouri. I have a son, Gordon Caldwell, and a daughter, Leslie Rodgers. I also have two grandsons, Robert Caldwell and Tory Rodgers. My life has meaning and is still filled with the sounds of *The Beatles* music!

Foundations

MARY JEAN EISENHOWER

It is fair to say Mary Jean Eisenhower did not have a typical childhood as the granddaughter of a United States President. Add the venerable Mamie Eisenhower for a grandmother, and life became "surreal" for this present-day humanitarian.

Life has also thrown its fair amount of obstacles in her path, including childhood polio, career problems and divorce. Still, she has achieved what many only dream.

Her work with People to People, the non-profit organization that assists those in need all over the world, has brought her face to face with her purpose in life. She considers herself lucky to have an opportunity to help others.

The Way I See It...

Other people mistake kindness with weakness. If you are a steel magnolia, you are kind and you are not the least bit weak.

Hear the Whispers

I was very coddled and protected as I was growing up. If I had a problem in school with someone I admired, I would tell my mom I couldn't wait to be a grown up, when everybody got along. Of course, it doesn't work that way. I learned some pretty brutal lessons in young adulthood that showed me the world wasn't perfect...my early "shock factor."

My dad, John Sheldon Eisenhower, is the son of Dwight Eisenhower, the 34th President of the United States. My mom, Barbara Jean Thompson, was a military brat who met my dad in Austria right after the war. They were married 34 years.

Daddy grew up an only child. His older brother passed away from scarlet fever while my grandmother, Mamie Eisenhower, was carrying my father. My mom was one of four children, which seemed to make up for daddy's lack of siblings. I am the youngest of four, which is a life lesson all by itself.

My grandfather was a knee-slapping grandfather, a regular family man. I found that trait so endearing. I didn't realize he was globally special until I entered school and people started treating me strangely. I knew he lived in a fancy house and he came home from the *office*. I just didn't connect the Oval Office with the presidency at the time. To the credit of my parents and grandparents, our lives were as normal as possible, but it was still surreal. Friends would ask me if I had a huge allowance as I was growing up. I told them my allowance came in the form of an after-school job! So there was normalcy, but I was also sheltered.

I would often wonder who my "Commander-in-Chief and President" grandfather really trusted. When my father graduated West Point on D-Day, he went to England to be my grandfather's aide throughout the war. So the answer was: you trust your family.

Growing up, I wanted to be like June Cleaver. I wanted a white picket fence and I wanted to clean the oven in my pearls! In reality, my mentor was my grandmother, Mamie. She was a steel magnolia, a grit. No question about it. A woman with a backbone doesn't forget how to be a woman: she knows how to be hard, but she realizes she's soft. Every woman needs to emulate a man's strength and still keep her softness and femininity. Other people mistake kindness with weakness. My grandmother, like a steel magnolia, showed kindness but was not the least bit weak.

After my grandparents retired to Gettysburg, we saw them every day because our property abutted their farm. We were a close-knit family. Not many people were as close to their grandparents as I was.

My mother stayed busy raising four children, but my grandparents always had time for me. This is oftentimes true with grandparents, especially when parents have a large family. My grandmother always had a minute to talk. After my grandfather passed away, I would see her on weekends because Gettysburg was only about an hour and fifteen minutes away from my house in D.C. By that time, my sisters and brothers were all married and I was the only unmarried one. I am so blessed to have spent that time with her.

When I was about to be married, she shared her checkbooks from the twenties to show how she budgeted during the Depression. I couldn't believe she still had them. She taught me etiquette and manners and "just how to be." She said it was "tacky to wear your diamonds before noon," so I don't wear my cubic zirconiums before noon!

The whole June Cleaver thing didn't work out for me. I had a couple of not-so-wonderful marriages but I have a fabulous son, so no complaints. I ended up an involuntary career girl, a different plan for me from the beginning. I worked with my current ex-husband at an engineering firm. I managed the money and he was the engineer. Working 70 hours a week, we raised his children and my son, who had a touch of dyslexia. While I cooked dinner, I helped my son with his homework. I went to school twice, once for him, as support, and once for myself. It was wearisome.

When I came into contact with People to People, it was almost an epiphany—totally unexpected. I met Sergei Khrushchev, the son of one of my grandfather's greatest adversaries, former Soviet Premier *Nikita Khrushchev*, at a People to People function. I had been invited to speak and was surprised they put the two of us together on the program. Sergei often speaks to American audiences to share his memories of the "other" side of the Cold War. As it turned out, he was one of the nicest people I had ever met.

Then, I saw it: the whole People to People thing. The stated purpose is to have international understanding and friendships through educational, cultural, and humanitarian activities. It was a very real concept and it worked. From that moment forward, I wanted nothing more than to go to work for People to People. I accepted an offer from the organization and moved to Kansas City. My marriage was falling apart at the time and this decision gave my life purpose. It was such a pleasant surprise. The puzzle started to make sense, and I landed in the shoes I was supposed to wear.

After this experience, I wouldn't know how to live any other way. I have been lucky to have the opportunity to make even a tiny impact on people's lives. Our organization works to bring peace around the world and we are involved in several humanitarian endeavors. People to People stations its employees in different countries where they work to make a difference. For example, we provide supply bags with toothbrushes and other essential supplies for the underserved. The people we work with honestly cannot afford these everyday items. Scores of underserved youth help us with our mission, thereby helping other underserved children.

A most bittersweet moment of courage happened for me in Jordan during the triple bombings in November of 2005. It was 11/9 instead of 9/11, which some believe was on purpose. Directly behind our hotel during a wedding ceremony, a bomb exploded. It was a nightmare...very graphic. Going to the bombing site and relating to what those victims must have gone through took me the longest time to get over.

Interesting for me, though, I learned what it takes to make peace. The Jordanian priest left his parish to sit with the Americans the next day to ease our fears. The Royal Family called to make sure we had what we needed and to reassure us that we would be fine. Jordan, of course, was closed. We were confined to the hotel at least for the first day for our own safety, so that the dust would settle. As Americans in a foreign country faced with something of this magnitude, we didn't know if we were the next statistic or not.

That whole experience taught me that peace and comfort *do* come into the world. People need to understand that fortunately, the really scary things do fail. What we don't hear, and maybe this is why they call it faith, are the beautiful things about the world—the priest who left his parish to sit with the Americans or the young men and women who risk their lives for others. It's not their battle, but they go fight it. These things are not printed in the newspaper. You have to trust and have faith that they exist and go find them for yourself.

One of my biggest lessons in life is "don't sweat the small stuff." I am a childhood polio survivor. I was one of the two percent who caught it from the vaccine. It was a mild case, leaving my left side with half the strength of my right side. I had special exercises for gym class up until the ninth grade. The teacher stayed after school every night to help bring me up to the level of the other kids. I found my way in that formal gym class in school and haven't missed a beat. I *will* say that I have had some pretty achy bones over the years. I had a surgical correction in 2005 that helped, but the week before the surgery, I had been feeling miserable. I was in Sri Lanka, right after the tsunami, to assess the situation on how to best use the money we had received for the victims. I started to hurt badly while I was there. Then I saw an amputee from a landmine. I thought to myself, "Never mind my pain." Don't sweat the small stuff.

Another defining moment happened while in Sri Lanka at a school. The people knew nothing about me except that I was western and my name was Mary. We arrived to make a donation and see what life was like for the kids. The school matron whispered to me that every child I was going to meet that day had parents who were killed in the civil war. Their ages ranged from one to twelve. A group of kindergarteners were waiting for me. As I came in, they clapped their hands and fell into the cross-legged position on the floor, singing *Mary had a Little Lamb*. I recognized the tune and I sat down cross-legged with them and started singing along in English. Those are the little things that last a lifetime and will perhaps allow me to leave my legacy as a friend who loved.

It took me a long time to accept the world as it is. If I had to live my life over, I would try to hear the "whispers." Sometimes, it's right there and you have no idea. John Lennon said, "Life usually happens when you're out planning something else." I love his lyrics: "Let there be peace on earth and let it begin with me." That is realistic...it's not just an idealistic song. It doesn't matter what the vehicle is for peace. It could be entertainment or a cultural exchange. It doesn't matter if we speak the same language. It doesn't matter that we dress differently. It doesn't matter that my god differs from your god, especially in today's world. We are not an island and people need to realize that. Not only realize it, but savor and cherish it.

"Don't compromise yourself. You are all you've got."

—Janis Joplin
(1943–1970) American singer, songwriter & music arranger

JANE M. PHILO

Jane Philo never dreamed she would be anything other than a nurse. To her amazement, she built the Gulf Coast Women's Center, a domestic violence shelter in Biloxi, Mississippi. When she retired, she had a staff of 40, served six counties and 400,000 people with a budget of $1.5 million.

In the early 1990s, it was not a crime for a husband to rape his wife in Mississippi. Jane worked 24/7 for 21 years, no vacations, never without a phone or pager, constantly on call—trying to give women their human rights.

As testimony to her service to the community, she was given a "day" by the Mayor's office. Countless numbers of people experience a better quality of life due to her service to the center. As a result, the building constructed during her leadership bears a plaque and dedication to Jane Philo "as a monument to her vision and guidance."

The Way I See It...
Social change is slow, but it has been my passion to push it along.

Bend the Old Rules
People think of the old days as fun loving and carefree, but where I grew up in Plattsburgh, New York, most families had one car and lived

in small apartments. Central air conditioning was a luxury and home ownership was for the well off. Women walked to the grocery and carried heavy bags home. Most of them didn't drive. Their social life was visiting with each other and they called each other "Mrs." First names were not used.

Growing up in the 1940s, women had few choices. Since it was expected that a woman would marry and leave the work force, there was no point in spending time or money for her to go to college.

Nursing looked to me as a way out of a typical typing job. I had to be self sufficient because family money or scholarships didn't exist for girls in upstate New York. I ranked second in my class and did athletic and extracurricular activities, but such achievements didn't equal success for a woman in those days.

I located a small college, acquired enough money to attend and after four years, I had a degree in nursing. I went looking for work. I didn't face challenges from men seeking the same jobs. I never saw any men! The pay was most likely too low for them and the title implied female. Men didn't want to do "women's work." Even today, men in the field of nursing still have a problem with it. Nurses were subordinate to physicians who were men. Finding work was relatively easy.

When I married my career Air Force husband, I was fortunate to continue finding work in nursing, particularly public health. We moved often and even spent two years in Turkey. I received my first masters in Counseling and Human Development before moving to Mississippi, where I decided to get another master's degree in Psychiatric and Mental Health Nursing. During school, I landed a part time counseling job at a domestic violence center in Biloxi. By the time I took the job, my position had turned into deputy director, then director. It was an immense job and it became the one I never left. It was my life.

One of the most important aspects of the center's program was trying to make a difference through the state legislature. Laws were on the books that needed to be changed. When legislation was finally introduced to make marital rape a crime, one particular legislator said that he didn't "really think it needed to be done because the man was just trying to go to a juke joint for a little fun and his wife wouldn't let him, so he probably had to get her out of the way." In other words, he beat her up to get out of the door.

The chair of the committee made his point. "It's quite often a wife experiences tearing of her vagina. In normal sexual relations within a marriage, women suffer vaginal lacerations." How he could make such a statement was beyond any reasonable person. Stranger still, his wife, a representative in the legislature, made no comment when he made the statement. I'm sure she wasn't too happy when his name and *their* phone number were printed in the paper.

The capital was overwhelmed with phone calls about this bill, so, of course, it passed and became law. We got back at him. Nevertheless, I was careful to avoid him except when I had to get bills through his committee. You never knew whether the legislators would retaliate if you upset one of them. The general consensus was that women shouldn't have certain rights…these rights only belonged to men.

When casino gambling won approval in Biloxi and our site was chosen for a new casino, we were forced to relocate our shelter. The gaming commission held a meeting with the casino management and ruled that all social services affected would be assisted with relocation by the casinos. The assistance didn't materialize. As a matter of fact, the casinos treated me and the shelter deplorably. One of their lawyers stated that I wanted a "Taj Mahal and her work doesn't deserve it." Another lawyer actually threatened me when I told him I would go public with his denial for assistance.

We fought many battles. We felt like an underground charity most of the time. Domestic abusers are everywhere and most of the opposition to our work was generally personal. We had a hard time getting people on board.

A municipal judge tried to bar our people from his court and when he couldn't do that, he wouldn't acknowledge them. He tried to keep public records from our staff. He advised domestic violence offenders not to plead guilty because Mississippi law would no longer allow them to carry a firearm. He did everything he could to destroy us. In meeting with him, he refused to listen. He told me my knowledge in the field wasn't important. Just prior to his leaving the bench, he referred to me as a radical. According to his sister and brother, they grew up in an abusive household.

On the floor of the U.S. House of Representatives, someone once said domestic violence shelters were run by lesbians for lesbians. When I returned to the coast, I had everyone call him and tell him that wasn't so.

One prominent man in our community said he wouldn't give to our organization if it had the word *woman* in its name. I heard later he beat his wife. Negative comments came from abused victims who oftentimes became abusers themselves. Situations like this were irritating and frustrating and only made our work more difficult and challenging.

Positive supporters championed our cause too. I was impressed when I met a new general and his wife who came to our nearby air force base. The general's wife told me she had once been married to an airline pilot who beat her. The general ended up one of our best supporters and was actually quoted in *Glamour* magazine advising women about domestic violence.

Women shared their stories of violence with me all the time. A reporter told me about her violence but said please don't tell anyone. I wondered, "Why not?" It wasn't her fault. Some women blame themselves—they feel that they aren't meeting the needs of men and have brought this awful thing on themselves. I didn't ask her about it or challenge her right to confidentiality. At some point, she'll come out and talk about it. It has to be her choice when to talk.

Social change is slow, but it has been my passion to push it along.

When I married, it was assumed that I would not work at all, or work only until children arrived. It would have been a terribly limiting existence for me, trapped in such a scenario. Sometimes I had to stop working because I had no childcare, but I never wanted to stop completely. I thought about switching careers when we could not afford to further my nursing studies or a transfer loomed for my husband. But things would always work out to keep me in Public Health. Now, I understand how my career path has afforded me the opportunity to fight and make a difference for women's human rights.

I learned how to bend the old rules.

"Talk about it only enough to do it. Dream about it enough to feel it.
Think about it only enough to understand it. Contemplate it only enough to be it."

—Jean Toomer
(1894–1967) American poet and novelist

NINON DE VERE DE ROSA

From an unusual, lonely and battered childhood, Ninon de Vere De Rosa became a self-made and internationally recognized businesswoman and motivational speaker.

When any door of opportunity presented itself, she walked right through it…and she is now a positive role model for people all over the world.

As founder and executive director of KidsTalk Foundation, Inc., her award-winning television show, Voices of Tomorrow, *has garnered more than 92 awards, including the Davey Award, Gracie Allen Award and 20 Telly Awards. She also founded the Hal Roach Awards for Loyola Marymount University which celebrates various Hollywood legends like Ralph Bellamy, Henry Mancini and Audrey Hepburn. As an actress in Europe, she starred as Rita Hayworth's stand-in.*

She has been personally honored by President George W. Bush, U.S. Senator Diane Feinstein, as well as others for her invaluable contributions to society and entrepreneurial spirit. Her life has been a series of overcoming obstacles successfully and she firmly believes in marching to the beat of her own drum.

The Way I See It...

Get to know your inner self. Attitude and perseverance can win out even among the most overwhelming odds.

Queen of the Kids

I had a different childhood…*very* different. I was one of five children in England, living in a place called Torquay Devon. I was born at home and, if the truth be known, we hardly ever left the house. My mother and father decided they didn't want any of us going to school or talking like other children or getting all "those colds." We weren't allowed to mix with other kids so we had no friends. At one point, we lived out on a cliff in a very small bungalow…nobody around for miles. It was very strange.

My education consisted of my parents sending me into a room with a book to read by myself. I hardly knew how. When they asked me questions about what I had read, they would get angry with me because I didn't know the answers. They would send me back into the room. I only had a couple of hours a day of "supposed" education, but not even every day.

It was a tough 16 years of my life, but I have an "energy" that allows me to create beautiful moments out of my childhood. As long as I have created beautiful memories, what does it really matter? I just keep pushing and going. I am the type of person who doesn't let people or things get in her way.

When I was 16 years old, I worked 20 hours a day for a whole year. Sundays, it was 18 hours. I saved 100 pounds, worth about $400 today. I would walk about two miles at six in the morning to work at a small hotel. We didn't have cars, only the bus system, but I couldn't afford the fare. The owners liked me because I worked and didn't just *pretend* to work. I ended up running the whole hotel. After a full day there, I would dash down and cashier at a ballroom till two in the morning. I was honest and they trusted me with money.

I had already left home and was supporting myself. My parents never got in touch with me to see if I was okay. At the time it did not bother me, but now I look back and wonder, what on earth were they thinking and how could they just leave me?

Next, I moved to London to live with my grandmother. I saved enough money for a photo portfolio for modeling. The pictures turned out well because I was hired and ended up becoming a well known model in London, Beirut and Europe. I was the first model to dance down an aisle! I always smiled too. Most models at that time were prim and proper walking down the aisle. Not me. I worked for Harrods of London's Lady Marlayne, Marks and Spencer and other big names in the business. I was in an underwater swimming act in Beirut, Lebanon with Charlie Henches, the Russian producer of "Mai Oui," one of the biggest shows in the world at the time. I didn't know what I was doing at the audition in London but I knew what he was looking for: I dove down into a large indoor swimming pool to where he was standing and smiled at him underwater. He gave me the job!

I was quite famous in England, going under my first and middle name, Ninon de Vere. It was part of my father's family name, still well known in England. I was not like other girls at all. I wanted to dress in expensive clothes but I did not have the money, so I would sew my own couture dresses. Although it seems contradictory, I was not obsessed with money. My goal was to succeed and be the best. I worked twice as hard as most people because I didn't have their education or knowledge. But my upbringing taught me how to deal with challenge. You don't have to know how to read or write, although it is better if you do. You can still make it. You can live in any country you want without knowing anybody. Language doesn't matter. People are people.

I am not a women's libber and I don't think we should be liberated from anything that we are. Men are men and we are women and we should be part of everything and everybody. Unfortunately, being an attractive woman with a personality can be an obstacle. Other women may feel you are a challenge. They don't want you with their men or in their circle. It is difficult to challenge yourself to succeed and then overcome the challenges of being a woman, *and* other women.

Since my husband died, I started my own real estate company. There are times when men don't take you seriously. If you go to lunch with a man, it isn't thought of as business. They will bring someone else along for backup in case someone says, "I saw your husband with a blonde." I will not let anyone tell me I can't have lunch with somebody because he is a "man." I march with a big stick to a different drummer. Women will not be second class. There are men and there are women…no first and second class.

In Europe, we are a little different. We know who we are and what role we play and we are very proud of it. In America, women seem to be insecure. They try to "get this guy" but not in the right way. Women who live in America should be proud of who they are. Honor yourself and you will be honored.

I could never have children because my husband had a vasectomy before I met him. We tried to reverse it, but it didn't work. I fell in love with him before I knew that. I also didn't know he had six children when I met him! There were challenges as a step mom. His children didn't like me and they treated me badly, always getting me into trouble over something I never said. He had no contact with three of them for some time and the other three did not live with him. I thought it would be nice for my husband to have his children around, so I brought them all back to their father, thinking that was the correct thing to do. I did not know the consequences. My philosophy was not to treat them badly just because they were doing it to me. I never told my husband. It would only create more problems. Sometimes it is better to keep your mouth shut. Remember God gave us two eyes, two ears, one nose with two nostrils and only one mouth! That has to tell you something, right?

I am a funny person. I don't like to see the ugly side of life. Life is too beautiful. God gave me 24 hours a day, light and dark, and the air to breathe. I try not to see negative things. That is why it was so painful when I reached my lowest point in life...when my husband, father and mother died.

Even though my husband and I were divorced, we were still close. He had a fear of dying young, since all his family had died at 62. I kept him alive and protected him and he lived to be 78, but he died exactly 10 months after he moved out of my house. His daughter had taken him away from me and did not take care of him. It was so sad. We were both still in love. He had dates and relationships with other women but I wasn't jealous. He had married very young and never had his play time. I didn't regret him having that time. The other women never lasted long.

One day, I had a vision of him not feeling well so I called to check on him. He said he was ill. He had gone to Las Vegas by himself. He was a big gambler and a drinker. He had two accidents going out there and two coming back and his head was hurting badly. I went over to see him. He was in a bad way with nobody taking care of him. I helped him and said I would be back. I called a few days later with no answer. I went to his house and he was not there. His lawyer friend had put him into the hospital. It was totally heartbreaking...the man I loved for 29 years...dying. The children had taken the love of my life away and this was the consequence. My beautiful stepdaughter had banned me from his hospital room. I never knew why and he died two weeks later. I did manage to see him right before he died, when they had pulled all the plugs. Nobody was with him.

Two weeks later, my father died of cancer in England.

Two months after that, my mother went into the hospital with a stroke and could not talk. She died a short time later. We had become very close in her last few years. She was my best friend.

Suddenly, I had no one to talk to. My strength was very low. Three of the most important people in my life were gone, but I had to keep moving forward because that was my tenacity from childhood. I had to make a living.

I had learned real estate over the years from my husband and decided that I wanted to make my own way. I didn't want a man coming into my life with his money and none of my own. Real estate has permitted me to pursue my passion: God allowing me to do what I need to do. You can't sit back and do nothing. You have to realize what is within you to move forward the right way.

I began to lose my identity during my marriage. I was making dinners and society was wonderful. I was floating along. I even founded the Hal Roach Awards for Loyola Marymount University and raised a tremendous amount of money for the University. But something was missing. I wasn't doing anything that I really wanted to do.

One day in the supermarket, I watched a woman yelling at her four-year-old child. I stood looking at them, thinking this child is so young and she can't defend herself—everyone is watching this woman embarrass her. That is why I started *KidsTalk*. I remembered getting yelled at and my father hitting me. I wrote *KidsTalk* in 1992 and in 1996 we produced our first show. I had done filming and acting but for the past 15 years, I had been a wife. Don't get me wrong…I had loved it! I met my husband with no money and we ended up with a $4 million home in Bel Air. Now I needed to focus on my purpose, and I wanted to do my show. The first show featured divorced families. The second was about the deaf and hearing impaired and that won my first award. Now we have over 400 shows. My whole purpose was to tell children they can have a voice in society and people will listen. My passion comes from my childhood. God didn't give me any children; He gave me a *world* of children.

If you stay focused long enough on whatever you want, you will get it. The challenge is living in this world and becoming someone. The only time you will not become someone is when you put a wall up. Nobody puts a wall up but you.

Today, I am on a platform that couldn't be greater. I want to build my empire as an individual woman. I feel it moving forward and I am very secure. People have trust in me. Of course, the proof is in the pudding…I have to let my people know I can do it. I *am* doing it and I am working hard.

"If you always do what interests *you*, at least one person is pleased."

—*Katharine Hepburn*
(1907–2003) American actress

TERRE THOMAS

Terre Thomas is no stranger to the entertainment business. Danny Thomas, her father, is the award winning comedian and founder of St. Jude Children's Research Hospital. Her sister Marlo is a famous actress and her brother Tony is a successful Hollywood producer. Terre also took her turn on stage as a singer, but she always knew that while music remained deep in her heart and soul, her true passion was children.

Today, she devotes her life not only to her family, but to the children of St. Jude. Terre would be the first to tell you that her purpose in life is not defined by fame and fortune, but by raising her two children and having them turn out to be such wonderful human beings.

The Way I See It...

True grit means withstanding...holding on when the tide comes in and tries to drag you down. It's about understanding and remembering your true purpose, especially when the waves are crashing in all around you. I have come to learn that there will always be something to knock you down; true grit is about not letting it break your spirit.

The Vow that Changed Our Lives

Danny Thomas knelt in a Detroit church in front of a statue of St. Jude Thaddeus, the patron saint of hopeless causes. He prayed for a sign. Should he stay in show business or change direction? Mom wanted him to do something secure like work in the produce business or in a grocery store because working as a comedian was so sporadic and unpredictable. Again, he prayed to St. Jude Thaddeus, "Help me find my way in life and I'll build you a shrine." He didn't have anything and wasn't sure what the shrine would be. He might be able to create a side altar or maybe even build a little clinic for children. One by one, he was shown signs that encouraged him to continue pursuing his dream of being an entertainer. Many people make hollow vows...not Daddy!

As his success grew, so did his passion for this project. Of course, at the time, he had no idea it would be such a monumental undertaking. Yet, he never lost sight of it and it became a passion for all of us in the family. As fate would have it, the hospital became the greatest pediatric cancer research hospital in the world.

Music was always such an important part of my life; maybe it was inherent because my parents met as singers on radio in Detroit. I was not interested in a full time career in music and life on the road. Who is to say that I would have had what it takes to make it, anyway? I wanted to have children more than anything and, luckily, I didn't have to choose between music and family. If I did, children would have won, hands down... no doubt about it! It was never a contest! My passion for children was a sure thing and I was not going to give that up. If you have music in your heart and soul, you can sing anywhere, even driving carpool. You don't need an audience. I shared the gift of music with my children and taught them my little acronym, GML—God, Music and Laughter—can get you through anything in life.

When St. Jude Children's Research Hospital opened in 1962 in Memphis, Tennessee, Daddy said, "Now I know why I was born." We were all so touched by his passion for this amazing facility and what it could accomplish. In a sense, we feel like we were born to carry on our dad's legacy. He never pushed it at us or dropped it on us, but it was one of the greatest gifts you could inherit...and clearly the right thing to do. Dad came to believe that his entire career was just a vehicle to take him to the place where he could do something lasting to help children. It was a God-given career that made it possible for doctors to do what they could to save children's lives.

Dad was Lebanese and Mom was Italian/Sicilian, so there was always activity and music in the house... noise and joviality, personalities vying for airspace at our dinner table—when you *got the floor,* you kept it as long as possible.

Dad was the most influential person in my life. Marlo and Tony feel the same way. He was just like he was on his TV show, *Make Room for Daddy.* Although he could be loud as a lion, he was always gentle as a lamb. He was family-minded. He came from a large family, nine boys and one girl. You can imagine what a saint my grandmother was! He always had time for us and came to everything we were involved in.

Mom was always such fun to be with—she had more energy than all of us. When we went to a restaurant, they would often play *Danny Boy* or *Rose Marie, I Love You.* Mom would tell jokes to the Italian waiters in Italian. They would encourage her to play the piano and sing. Dad would proudly sit there with an unlit cigar in his mouth. Mom *was* the proverbial wind beneath Dad's wings. He asked Jim Weatherly to write a song about Mom. He wrote *You're the Best Thing That Ever Happened To Me.* Ray Price and Gladys Knight both sang it. They each had great success with the song—a great tribute to Mom.

It was hard when Mom got dementia about six years after Daddy went to heaven. Although she had a nurse, I was always there. She had taken care of me and I was going to do the same for her. It's the hardest thing to see someone who was so vibrant lose herself. Failing health is so hard to accept.

I, too, had run-ins with Mother Nature. It started right after the birth of my second child, with the discovery of a little blue knot right below my right knee. I didn't think much of it at first. I had it for years and assumed it was a bruise from playing on the floor with my daughter or kneeling at church or hitting it on a cabinet. When it started growing, I had it checked out. No one thought it was anything. You have to be your own doctor much of the time and I felt something wasn't right. Finally, a great surgeon told me it was a blue nevus tumor, a second-degree melanoma. He said if the cancer spread at all, I could die in about a month. I said, "I'm not going to die. I just had my son 10 months ago, and I have a 3 ½ year old daughter at home, and I'm going to raise them." The surgery to remove it was successful. The tumor had remarkably stayed intact after all those years. I truly believed I had been given a second lease on life.

About 30 years later, doctors found a growth on one of my ovaries. They advised me to have surgery to remove the growth, even though they felt certain it was benign. My decision to have the surgery was confirmed when just days before the operation, my daughter told me she was expecting *my first grandchild*. I wanted to have the surgery and get it over with; I felt a peace that everything would be fine. The surgery was a complete success—the growth was benign.

Years later, out of nowhere, an *innocent* cough led my brilliant doctor to suggest a cat scan. The results confirmed that I had another cancer. This time it was a small tumor in the lung. We found it early and I didn't have to have chemo and radiation. My parents must have been *nagging* God!

It's funny how we can obsess endlessly over the small things, but learn quickly to accept the big things. We need to look to a purpose bigger than ourselves and work every day for that purpose. For me, I have my children and my grandchildren, and I have St. Jude Children's Research Hospital. They keep me going…and going…and going.

My faith and the Book of Proverbs have helped me through the toughest times of my life. Proverbs 3:5 says, "Trust the Lord with all your heart and lean not on your own understanding." There is no way we can understand why tough times come. What I do know is we can count on God's presence and guidance—that's a big source of my strength.

I learned about giving and making an impact on my community from my dad. He wanted to help as many people as he could. He showed me how important each individual is to any cause, and that was empowering to me. Thinking of his hospital, he would say that it is the small donor that runs it. It's like an adage I once heard, "Drop by drop makes the lake." The research at St. Jude affects the world. Daddy used to say, "The entire pediatric community of the world looks to St. Jude, in Memphis, Tennessee, for the answers in childhood cancers and catastrophic diseases." I can hear him say that like it was yesterday.

I would say to any young woman today who is trying to make her way—beginning her journey—simply be your own person and be the best at whatever you are going to be. Don't lean on a man, or anyone, too hard. Don't depend on another person to be your only source of happiness or to make you feel complete. Believe in yourself and *be* yourself... and you will make it. And, don't forget... GML.

My children were my biggest goal and they are my greatest achievement. I was *successful* in raising two responsible young people who are now out in the world, affecting others. They are so talented, and I'm so proud of them. They both have careers in show business where they have learned that getting to your goal is like walking in quick sand. They understand that show business is not always a choice, but more of a calling, and if you are in it for vanity, you won't last. Like their grandfather, their achievement and their grounded approach to their work is what they pass on to others.

"When the journey ends, it is the stories that remain.
These stories bring life and meaning to the journey."

—*Kitty Yucha*
Therapist & Homemaker, Florida

YOU PAVED THE WAY

There was no one there to show you
You had to find it on your own
A world that wanted to control you
Fed your resolve to overcome
You believed that voice inside you
More than the multitudes of doubt
And that's what separates
The ordinary from the great
A whisper from a shout

Don't matter what people say
You do it, your own way
With style and a woman's grace
Conviction, clear vision, true grit
Impassioned with courage, hope and faith
You paved the way

When I can't seem to move that mountain
Or walk through the lion's den
I look to you for inspiration
And find the strength that lies within
To reach a little higher
Than I ever thought I could
I'm willing to risk it all, knowing
That you have gone before me
So I can stand where you've stood

Don't matter what people say
You do it, your own way
With style and a woman's grace
Conviction, clear vision, true grit
Impassioned with courage, hope and faith
You paved the way

c. 2010 Rickles, Hargrove, Harris, Waldron. Vicki Rickles [Vick's Picks Publishing/BMI]; Jack Hargrove [Vick's Picks Publishing/BMI];
Ashley Harris [Revitalize Publishing/BMI] (www.ashleyharris.com); Mark Waldron [Acoustic Scribbles Music/BMI] (www.acousticscribbles.com)

To hear Ashley Harris sing **You Paved the Way**, written especially for **Women of True Grit**,
download it for free at www.womenoftruegrit.com or www.ediehand.com

Edie Hand's latest books:

Cancer: The Unexpected Gift

A Christmas Ride: The Miracle of the lights

The Soldier's Ride

The Last Christmas Ride

Genuine Elvis

Cajun and Creole Cooking with Miss Edie and The Colonel

Fall 2010:

ABC'S of Selling with Business Etiquette

About the Authors

EDIE HAND'S philosophy for living life with gusto can be seen in everything she does from her work as an acclaimed celebrity chef, author, philanthropist, speaker and business woman.

Edie learned about the simple joys of family, life and helping others from her modest childhood growing up in the rural south. She is a cousin to the late Elvis Presley and recently co-authored *The Genuine Elvis*. Edie understands tragedy with the loss of her three young brothers. She is also a three-time cancer survivor. Her gift to rise from tragedies to triumphs is evident in her life's work. She has authored, co-authored, and helped to develop over twenty books. Her other books include inspirational cookbooks, novellas and, stories of the heart with humor. They are all written from a strong woman's perspective.

Edie has starred in national commercials and daytime television soaps. She has hosted numerous national radio and television shows in her broadcasting career. She has been the CEO of Hand 'N Hand Advertising, Inc. since 1976.

Edie is actively involved with American Women in Radio and Television and the National Speakers Association. The Edie Hand Foundation works to benefit the Children's Hospital of Alabama, Children's Miracle Network, St. Jude Children's Research Hospital, and the Country Music Hall of Fame and Museum.

Edie is an alumna of the University of North Alabama. She currently lives near Birmingham, Alabama with her husband Mark Aldridge. Her only son, Linc Hand, lives in Los Angeles, California.

For more information go to these websites:

www.ediehand.com

www.ediehandfoundation.org

TINA SAVAS is among the first wave of women entrepreneurs in Birmingham, Alabama. In 1983, she founded the *Birmingham Business Journal* newspaper, followed by *Alabama Health News, Alabama Construction News,* and *Birmingham Weekly,* the area's only weekly alternative newspaper and continual winner of national editorial awards.

The *Birmingham Business Journal* was instrumental in changing the business landscape in Birmingham with in-depth business news never seen before. It was an uphill battle for a single woman in her twenties with little money in a tough industry, but Savas' determination won the day.

Her newspaper legacies include "The Fifty Richest" series, naming the area's 50 richest people and their net worth; "The Birmingham 100," listing the top private companies and their revenues; the "Top 40 Under 40" series, naming the up and coming stars all under the age of 40 (now copied in all U.S. major markets); the "Fast Track 25," ranking the fastest growing companies in the area; and the "Best in Business" awards.

She also created the "Top Birmingham Women" award, naming ten women each year who personify the highest echelons in the community. As a tribute to her, the *Birmingham Business Journal* presented Savas this award after she sold that publication.

She has served on local boards for community development, advised numerous foundations, colleges and hospitals and won many awards during her career. She hosted a weekly radio show, appeared on local television shows and is featured in the book, *Italians in the Deep South,* as one of the "newer generation" of Italians making "waves."

Savas continues her entrepreneurial spirit through real estate investment and other business ventures. Her passion for business has recently extended to volunteer and community work for those ages 50 and older. She lives in Birmingham, Alabama with her husband, Paul, and son, Alex.

For more information go to this website:
www.womenoftruegrit.com

Photography by Chris Savas | www.chrissavas.com